STER.

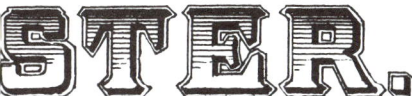

LITH & PUB. BOSTON.

17 NORTH SCHOOLBUILDING.
18 SOUTH " "
19 EAST LANCASTER SCHOOL BUILDING.
20 BENT WORKS. NEIL, TIPPET & KILLIAN.
21 BRIDGE SHOP: AUG. BORNEMAN.
22 R R SHOPS.
23 LANCASTER FOUNDRY & MACHINE SHOP.
24 EAGLE WORKS. MFC.

25 GRACE REFORMED CHURCH.
26 WOOLEN MILLS.
27 FLOURING MILL
28 JAIL.
29 MT PLEASANT.
30 FAIR GROUNDS (STATE & COUNTY)
31 BOARDING HOUSE J. KENNARD.
32 DR. NOURSE, OFFICE.

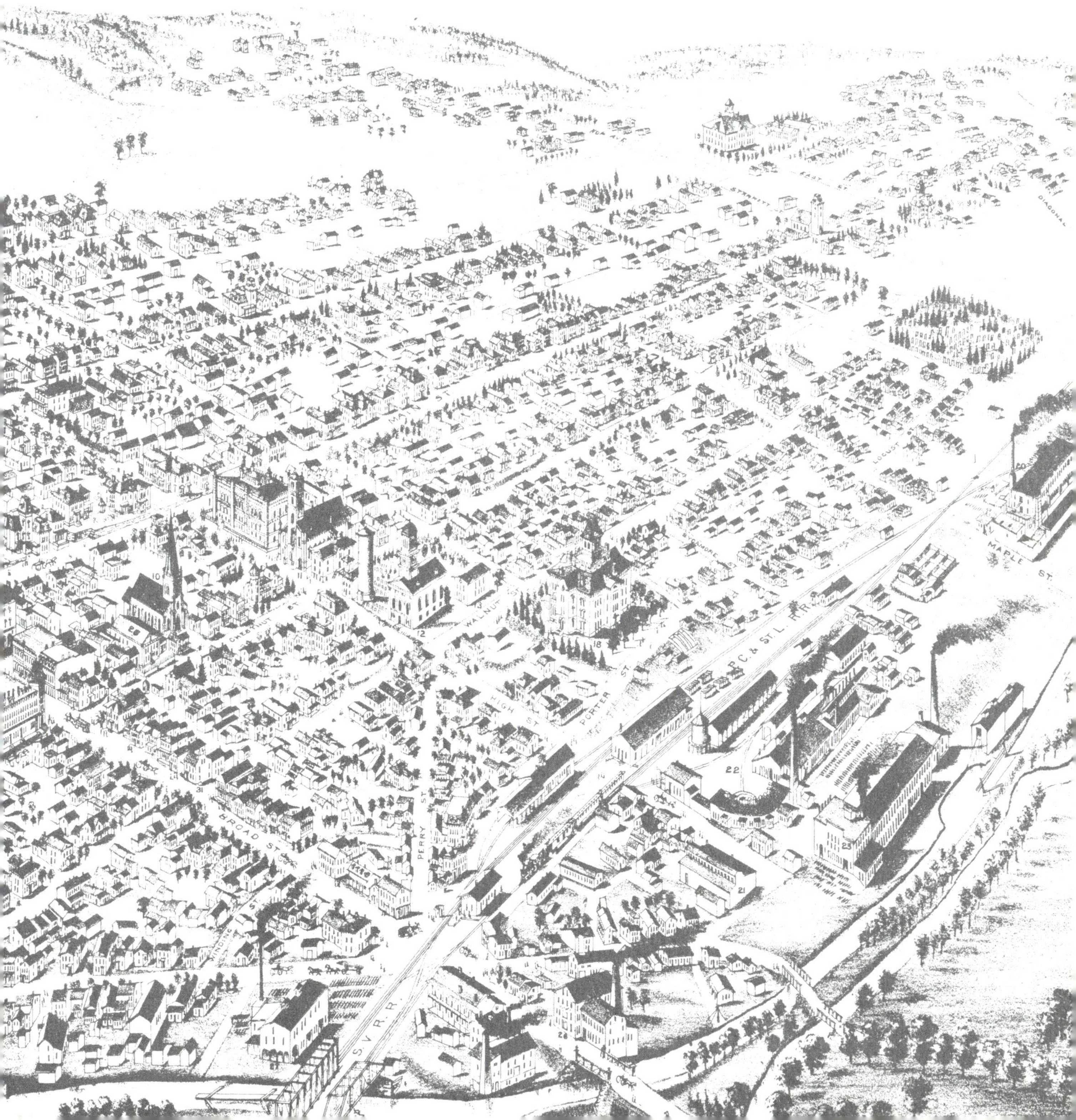

Heritage of
ARCHITECTURE and ARTS
Fairfield County, Ohio

by
Ruth Wolfley Drinkle

Second Edition

Photography
by
Judy Morehead and Nancy Wells Farrar

Editor's Note

This up-dated Second Edition of *Heritage of Architecture and Arts, Fairfield County, Ohio* remains the lively classic that Ruth Drinkle wrote in 1978, reflecting her tremendous knowledge and interest in her adopted home, and her very readable and individual style. Ownership information and photographs have been replaced as needed to record changes which have occurred since the original publication. Where owner's name is listed, the original owner (if known) is the first name listed, then the 1978 owner, then the 1994 owner at the time of printing. The editor and photographers of the First Edition have again worked on the Second Edition, keeping as a standard the preservation of the spirit of Ruth Drinkle, whose death in 1993 marked the end of an era for Fairfield County historians.

Copyright 1994 by the Fairfield Heritage Association, Inc. All rights reserved.

No parts of this book may be reproduced in any form or by any means without permission from the publisher.

Library of Congress catalog card number: 94-061293

Printed in the United States of America by Pfeifer Printing Company

Format design by Patricia Au and Karen Henry

ISBN-0-9602526-3-0

First Edition:

DEDICATED

to

CHARLES

*who brought me to Fairfield County, and whose
knowledge of history, whose understanding and
patience have been most helpful
in the preparation of this book.*

Second Edition:

DEDICATED

TO

the memory of

RUTH WOLFLEY DRINKLE

*a woman of remarkable curiosity, intelligence and
determination who gave so much to Fairfield County and
to the hundreds of people with whom she generously and
enthusiastically shared her knowledge and her love.*

Acknowledgements, 1978

We are particularly grateful to the many people in Fairfield County who so graciously cooperated with the Fairfield Heritage Association by permitting us to photograph their homes and their precious antique artifacts of local origin. Unfortunately, there are so many that it would be impossible to list them all. We are also very grateful to the Ohio Arts Council for the grant which made it possible to undertake this large project.

But we must give special recognition to the following people who have *volunteered* much time, supplied helpful information, or loaned particularly rare pictures to make this book more meaningful.

> Josephine Voss – Editor
> Jean Stuck – Business Manager
> Julie Scamehorn
> Linda Foor
> George Matchneer
> Duke Ellis
> David Contosta
> Mary Jane Outcault Pershing
> Dorothy Ent Coleman
> Charles Goslin
> Herbert Turner
> George Rising
> Herb Schumacher
> Paul Hanna
> Dr. Hubert Eyman, Jr.
> Phillip Leitnaker

Second Edition, additional acknowledgements, 1994

> Josephine Voss – Editor
> Nancy Farrar
> Jack Farrar, Farrar Photography
> Judy Morehead
> Mary Alice Drinkle Kuhn
> Charles H. Drinkle, Jr.
> Lorraine Arnold
> Pat Brown
> Debbie Rockwood

"A people which take no pride in the achievements of remote ancestors, will never achieve anything to be remembered by remote descendents" . . . . T. B. Macauly, and used by Hervey Scott to introduce his 1876 *History of Fairfield County*.

Table of Contents

Acknowledgments v
Preface-by David Contosta Ph. D. .... ix-x
Fairfield Frontier 1797-1815 .... p. 1-34
Classic Era, 1815-1840 .... p. 35-112
    Georgian
    Federal
    Greek Revival
Romantic Era, 1840-1870 .... p. 113-162
    Gothic Revival
    Italianate
    Second Empire
Late Victorian Era, 1870-1900 .... p. 163-179
    Picturesque Eclecticism
    Neo Classic Revival
    Richardson Romanesque

Bibliography .... p. 181
Index .... p. 183-186

PREFACE

At some time in our lives we realize in one way or another that we are creatures of the past. Relatives have told us that we have Great-Aunt Mary's eyes or that our musical ability must come from Grandfather Smith. In fact we are living testaments to the genetic and environmental impress of our ancestors, going back ultimately to the dawn of man.

Communities and even whole nations are likewise products of the past. Their languages, their religions, their political systems, and their aesthetic tastes all have developed over time. Indeed, the very existence of communal or national spirit depends upon the sense of a shared past, upon the memories of group hopes and fears, successes and failures.

In order to understand ourselves better as individuals or as members of a larger circle, we must never forget that we are not children of a day, of a month, or even of a year. Searching for individual identity, we thus consult older relatives and friends, genealogical records, or the papers and memorabilia of those departed. When seeking to grasp the meaning of our communal lives, we resort to public records or written histories. Just as important as these, however, are the buildings, furniture, and tools which prior generations have left. They form the most visible documents of our past and can tell us as much about ourselves as family trees, private diaries, or public documents. The art and architecture of nineteenth-century Fairfield County are no exceptions. If we will only look at them with open and informed eyes, they can reveal much about the development of our community and about its place in the nation at large.

The houses, furnishings, and implements of Fairfield County, for example, betray much of the area's natural history. Carpenters and cabinet makers transformed a wide variety of trees into clapboard, chests, hay rakes, door jambs, and fancy mantel pieces. Brick makers, stone cutters, and builders moulded the county's dull red clay and multi-colored sandstone into foundations, walls, and lintels. Thus if all the forests, together with the earth's upper strata were to disappear, we could reconstruct both from descriptions of nineteenth-century houses and their contents.

The architecture and arts of Fairfield County also reveal an abundance of information about the geographical and ethnic origins of area inhabitants. A colorfully painted Pennsylvania Dutch chair attests to the county's early German population and reminds us that Lancaster, the county seat, takes it name from Lancaster County, Pennsylvania, in the heart of the "Dutch country." Looking at the serpentine walls of several Lancaster dwellings, we are reminded of early nineteenth-century Boston and of the county's New England immigrants. The symmetrical and evenly spaced outbuildings of other residences bespeak Virginia origins and tastes.

Other facets of the region's art and architecture chronicle our economic development. Testifying to the county's moderate and steady growth are the solidity and modest scale of churches and public buildings. The relative absence of grandiose private mansions likewise signals an even, modest wealth in contrast to the domestic opulence of larger and wealthier communities. In reality, the very survival of so many edifices from the nineteenth century is owed to the lack of rapid economic growth. For the greatest enemy to antique architecture has been extraordinary commercial expansion, promoters destroying older buildings in the name of progress and efficiency.

Finally, the artistic documents of Lancaster and Fairfield County convey to us much about the wider currents of American thought and culture in the nineteenth century. In the late Georgian decoration of certain houses we find visible links to Baroque England as well as to colonial America. The county's

Federal dwellings and furniture reflect our founding fathers' dedication to the enlightenment qualities of balance, order, and harmony, while Lancaster's Greek Revival houses remind us of the early republic's admiration of ancient Greek democracy and culture. Through the Gothic Revival we gain insight into various aspects of the romantic era: it's religious fervor; its admiration for the middle ages; and its rejection of the geometric forms of the eighteenth century. The Mansard, Italianate, Romanesque, and eclectic styles bear witness to the later nineteenth century's continuing interest in the picturesque and far away, in addition to Americans' wider travel experiences.

The county is well endowed with excellent examples of these major styles and in Lancaster particularly we can examine all of them within the radius of a few blocks. A short walk around the city's central district is enough to introduce us to this unique heritage. It is my hope that the following pages will make us more aware of this inheritance and will reinforce our efforts to preserve what our ancestors, have left behind. In so doing we cannot fail to learn more about ourselves, our community, and our nation.

David R. Contosta, Ph. D.
Assistant Professor
Director of American Studies
Chestnut Hill College
Philadelphia, Pennsylvania

July 1978

PREFACE
TO THE SECOND EDITION

In the sixteen years since I wrote my Preface to the first edition of *Heritage of Architecture and Arts,* I have grown ever certain about the importance of history. For all knowledge of the past: We are too immersed in the feeling present to grasp its meaning, while the future is yet to come.

An appreciation for the past is also critical at a time such as ours when community identity continues to be eroded by modern technology. The ubiquitous and irreplaceable automobile has given birth to thousands of miles of shopping centers, at the same time that it has sucked the life out of downtowns all over the nation. Meanwhile, our modern chariots have sent citizens sprawling ever outward into suburbs that are further and further removed from the work place – or from any kind of commercial center. Then there are the video and computer revolutions that educate and amuse us at home, without resort to the theaters, clubs, and civic groups that once provided the bulk of our recreation and cultural uplift – and brought us face to face in the process.

In our fragmented age, this republication of the history of architecture and art in Fairfield County, Ohio may help to reinforce a sense of community pride as the twentieth century comes to an end, and as Lancaster moves toward its bicentennial in the year 2000. Most of all, it is a great tribute to its author, the late Ruth Drinkle, a devoted friend and source of inspiration to all who have labored to preserve our local heritage.

David R. Contosta

July 1994

Fairfield Frontier

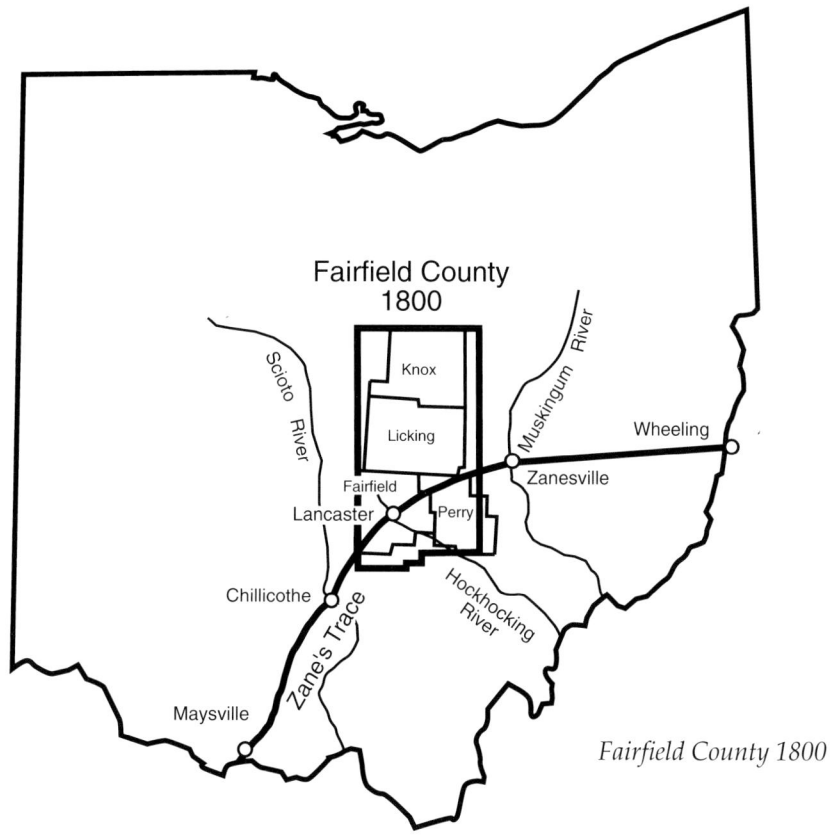

Fairfield County 1800

In May 1796, at the suggestion of Governor Arthur St. Clair, Congress determined to have a roadway built through a section of the vast and thinly settled Northwest Territory, in order to shorten the distance to some of its more remote parts. Heretofore, the only available routes had been by river and stream. Therefore, Congress obtained the services of Ebenezer Zane and his brothers Jonathon and Noah, early hunters, scouts and prospectors who had previously surveyed and blazed a road from Pittsburgh to Wheeling, to blaze a trail cross country from Wheeling, Va. to Limestone, Kentucky. For this service, the Zanes were to receive three square miles of land, one each on the Muskingum, the Hockhocking and the Scioto Rivers.

The Ordinance of 1787, with its four arresting and at the time revolutionary tenets (1) political freedom, (2) religious liberty, (3) prohibition of slavery, and (4) advancement in education, was an exceptional motivating power, which almost magnetically drew European as well as American guild-trained craftsmen and agriculturists to this section of the country. They came from the British Isles, Germany, Switzerland, Holland, France and Scandinavia and from nearly all of our seaboard states, but *primarily* from eastern Pennsylvania and Maryland.

Typical of the first cabins erected in Fairfield County by the earliest settlers, this log cabin was moved to the Fairgrounds in 1950, to show present and future generations the manner in which their forefathers lived. It is open to the public during the County Fair and on other special occasions. It has now been covered with exterior siding to protect its hand hewn logs from further deterioration.

Settlers coming west over Zane's Trace to stake claims in the Congress Lands of Ohio judged the desirability of the land by the lushness of the tree growth and the presence of good spring water. Fairfield County was covered by a luxurious stand of forest timber consisting of several varieties of oak, black and white walnut, elm, sugar maple, honey locust, buckeye, wild cherry and hickory. Paw paw, wild plum, maple, blackhaw, grapevine and spice bush made up a thickly set undergrowth. In the southern hilly part of the county, growths of pine with occasional stands of wild rhododenron and mountain laurel were also found, making a colorful pageant in the autumn, and in the Spring, blossoms and wild flowers of many kinds abounded.

Steeple notch construction, with wood and mud chinking was used in most of the log structures in Fairfield County.

Trestle table, treenware, flax wheel, and corner cupboard were typical furnishings of an early cabin.

The interior of this cabin, showing the large cooking and heating fireplace, exhibits many of the tools needed, and often made, by the first settlers – a wooden shovel, various axes, candle moulds, the ever-ready gun and powder horn. A reflecting oven, the trestle table, and the lovely little settee are a few of the first amenities of pioneer life.

For the earliest settlers, the trees supplied abundant material for their first homes and the furnishings therein. The first known of these "bold and enterprising" pioneers was Captain Joseph Hunter, who, with his family, emigrated from Kentucky in April 1798, and erected his log cabin on the prairie near the banks of the Hockhocking River. At that time, he had not a neighbor nearer than the Muskingum and Scioto Rivers, roughly thirty miles away. A son born to the Hunters, whom they named Hocking, was thought to be the first pioneer child born in Fairfield County. In the Spring of the same year (1798) Nathaniel Wilson, John and Allen Green, Joseph McMullen, Robert Cooper and Isaac Shaeffer also reached this valley, erected cabins and put in crops. In 1799 a tide of immigration set in with great force, with small settlements in Greenfield Township, on Rushcreek, Fetters Run, Raccoon and Pleasant Run, Toby Town, Muddy Prairie and Clear Creek. In April 1799, Samuel Coates, Sr. and Samuel Coates, Jr., coming from England, built a cabin where Zane's Trace crossed the Hockhocking, and started a mail route along the Trace from Wheeling, Virginia to Limestone, Kentucky!

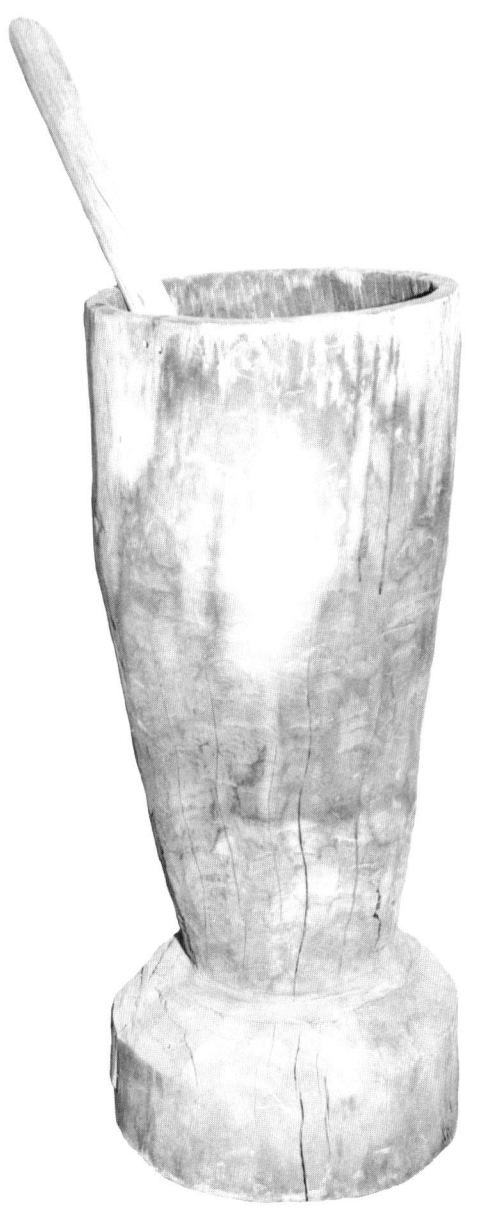

A rare hominy block was crudely fashioned from a tree trunk, by an early settler. It was used, like a mortar and pestle, to pound out corn for making johnny cake and corn pone, before grist mills were available.

This early cabin, constructed of white oak steeple-notched logs, originally stood on Bauman Hill Road. It was recently moved, reconstructed and authentically furnished by Max Stebelton. The hand hewn ceiling beams are hickory.

Inside we see a primitive bed, with a small trunk and a few pieces of furniture probably brought along over the mountains.

Completely modern 1825 kitchen of the Stebelton cabin, well equipped with hand forged iron cranes, hooks, and kettles of various sizes.

Along Zane's Trace stands this two story log house, probably built about 1829. The stone chimney has been rebuilt and the house has been adapted for present occupancy. Nearby is a deep well, 60 feet deep – much of it through solid rock.

A primitive drying rack was used both to dry herbs and some food products, and to harden candles.

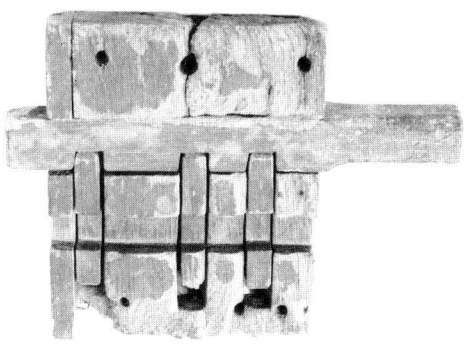

This primitive hand fashioned bolt lock was originally used to secure a smoke house. Here we see it in locked position. When the wooden key is inserted and turned, the wooden notches withdraw from the slots in the bolt, and the door is unlocked.

A cannonball four poster bed, with its trundle bed to accommodate some of the children, can here be seen. The hand woven coverlet was locally made. Beside the bed is the early candle stand holding the Bible.

The mail was carried by young boys on horseback through the long stretches of virgin forest. The first boy to carry the mail was George Sanderson. When he was but twelve years old he traversed the route over Zane's Trace (which at that time was little more than a blazed path) from Zanesville to Chillicothe once a week. Carrying the mail in saddlebags, he announced his welcome arrival at each settlement by blowing a blast on a long tin horn which he carried slung over his shoulder. This was the first *established* mail route through the interior of the Northwest Territory, and Samuel Coates, Sr. was the first postmaster in the new settlement.

Also in 1799, along with some neighbors from Westmoreland County, Pa., Frederick Harmon joined the emigration to the "west". Staking out his claim for 640 acres of land near New Lancaster, he walked back to Pennsylvania (his horse having been stolen by Indians), and later returned with his family in a Conestoga wagon, bringing with them a few prized possessions. Other household necessities had to be made as they were needed.

A rush bottom ladder-back chair which came into Fairfield County with the Harmon family.

Early wooden utensils, a butter paddle, shovel and bowl were made by a pioneer settler, and at a later date made into decorative objects by an unknown artist who painted primitive local scenes upon them.

This two and a half story log cabin, erected in 1802, and covered with walnut siding fifty years later is occupied by descendants of Frederick Harmon who built it. While the original outside steps to the second floor have been removed and an addition to enlarge the house has been made, it is otherwise much the same. It is interesting to note that this log cabin never had a fireplace.

Harmon-George 1802

The partitions inside the Harmon cabin are of wide wild cherry boards. The log construction can be seen in several places inside the house.

The two story log cabin built in 1802 by Frederick Harmon still stands and has been lived in continuously by his descendants. It originally had an outside stair, the only means of getting upstairs. Running barefoot outside, often on a snowy winter evening, to go up to bed made a vivid impression and memory for some of the "youngsters" of the family. After fifty years the Harmon family added several rooms and put walnut siding over the logs, and it has remained thus for over 125 years. Inside, the partitions between rooms are made of solid wild cherry boards. Until 1968 the original log saddlebag barn, which had about 135 logs 60 to 70 feet long, stood nearby, housing the conestoga wagon. Unfortunately it burned at that time. The three springs, which determined the location of the house, still run clear and strong. Nearby on ground given by Frederick Harmon is the Pleasant Hill Church and early graveyard where most of the Harmon descendants and deceased members of neighboring families are buried.

Had Frederick Harmon and his wife taken their son George on a Sabbath afternoon walk to the top of nearby Standing Stone in 1802 they, like Conrad Richter's characters who settled near Zane's Trace in *The Awakening Land*, might have looked down . . . "from the high pile of rocks on the settlement of Lancaster Town, with twelve or fourteen houses, not counting barns and outhouses. All had paths, or at least a line of flitched trees running between so women and young ones wouldn't get lost visiting a neighbor."

Since the dedication of New Lancaster in November 1800, work progressed so rapidly that by the Spring of 1801 streets and alleys in the central part of town assumed the shape they still retain. For the earliest settlers life was not easy – they had to rely upon themselves or what help they might get from neighbors, for shelter, for food, and for clothing. Their day was from sun-up to sundown. For a bit of light in their cabins they used betty lamps or occasionally a standing lamp with grease or a candle for fuel.

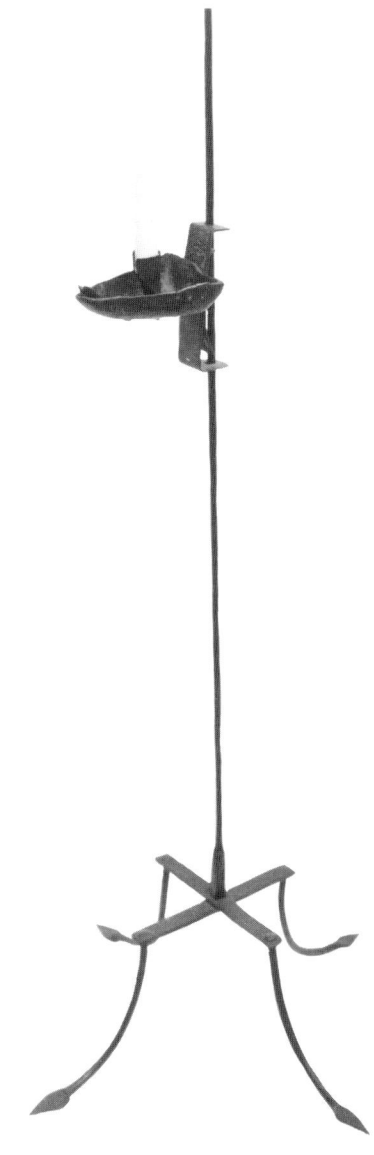

Occasionally there were standing lamps made. This particularly nice one could be adjusted as to height, and could use either grease with a wick or a candle, if available.

The earliest lighting devices used by the pioneers were betty lamps, which were easily transported, could be stuck into a log, and utilized grease for fuel.

An interesting and early vertical flax breaker.

A fine early spinning wheel, with flax in place, was locally made and has descended in the family of its orignal owner.

While the men and boys were busy clearing the land, planting and tending crops and hunting for game, the women and young girls early learned to spin and weave. They made their cloth from wool and flax (linsey-woolsey) and then fashioned it into their garments. They often made their own dye from native plants to add a bit of color.

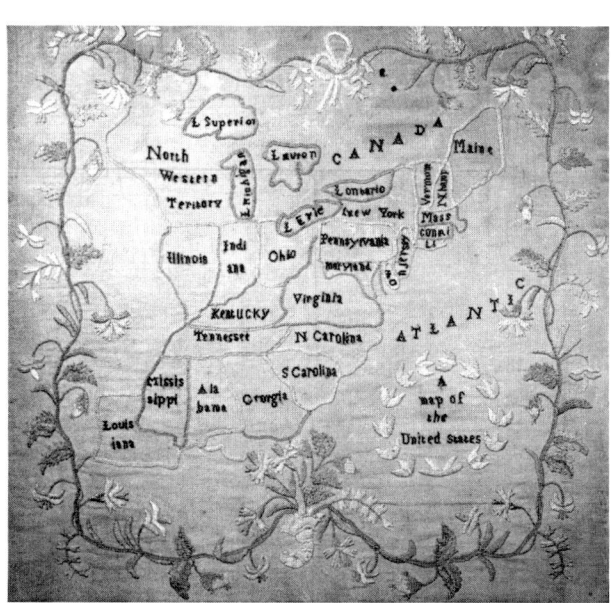

An early embroidered map – silk thread on linen - was "Wrought by Miss Agnes McCandish, Va". Her family came early to Fairfield County.

A sampler by "Elizabeth Arnold – her work – done in the eleventh year of her age – April 2, 1810" is executed in various colored silk thread on hand loomed linen. Little Miss Arnold later married Dr. Robert McNeil and they became very prominent citizens of Fairfield County.

It was considered a necessity for young ladies to learn fine needlework, usually starting with a sampler to practice different kinds of stitches and lettering. Soon they would learn to make quilts and more elaborate needlework, often displaying much creativity in their design and execution.

The deep religious beliefs of these earliest settlers sustained them through many hardships, and before they had time to build churches, religious services were held in their cabins. For this purpose Mary Noble loaned a tilt top candlestand, brought by her family from Maryland, to be used to hold the Bible as the focal point of such services. This candlestand was carried from one cabin to another for worship services.

In 1799, the Reverend James Quinn, a Methodist from Washington, Pennsylvania, made a missionary trip to the Hocking Valley. He brought his bride, Patience Teal of Baltimore, Maryland and they served the Hockhocking Circuit for many years.

The Reverend John Wright was also an early Presbyterian missionary, coming to Fairfield County early in 1801, serving stations in Rushville and Lancaster.

From the earliest times Methodist services, Lutheran services and Catholic services as well as Mennonite classes were held in cabin — according to the owner's beliefs — until 1806 when the first Court House was built, which then was also used as a central meeting place for religious services of various denominations.

It is interesting to note that many of the early missionaries or "circuit riders" also plied a trade to support themselves. Thus, James Finley, one of the earliest Methodist "circuit riders", is also listed as a silver smith.

This cherry candle stand brought from Maryland by the Noble family was loaned by them to the Presbyterians to be carried from cabin to cabin to hold the Bible for religious services – before any churches were built. The large family Bible was often the only, and certainly the most important book in each household. Here, beside the inspiration gained from the Holy Scriptures, family records of births and deaths, and marriages were carefully kept.

This early country church is typical of those built after the first log structures. Also typical is the adjoining grave yard, where many of those courageous early settlers were buried.

The first Court House, built in 1806, was a fine example of Federal architecture. Taken just prior to its demolition, this picture gives an idea of the earliest builders' knowledge of classical construction, with its symmetry, fine detailing, window treatment and interesting belfry.

Of the early craftsmen who settled here, Sothenes McCabe, was one of the first, coming in 1801. A brick maker and mason, he found clay suitable for making bricks. Undoubtedly he was first employed constructing more nearly fireproof chimneys to replace those first made of logs and mud, a cause of frequent fires.

But it was not long before brick buildings were being built in Lancaster (the "New" was dropped in 1803). As early as 1806 the first Court House, a neat structure of brick, was built near the center of Zane Square, at the intersection of Broad and Main Street. With its cupola belfry, this early Federal building was similar in style to the first Capitol in Chillicothe and reminiscent of many such structures back east. General John Williamson and James Hampson were the builders, with bricks manufactured by McCabe, who also supplied the bricks for the first few brick homes.

Now known as the Matlack house, this 1807 small brick cottage has been quite authentically restored. Its twelve over eight window panes, a simple walnut mantel with a wooden sink and open storage shelves, and a steep stairway to the two upstairs rooms (showing traces of the original green paint) are typical of the earliest houses.

The first fine brick residence was built at about the same time for Philemon Beecher, who had come here from Litchfield, Conn. to practice law. It was in his office that young Thomas Ewing (later to become a nationally known attorney and statesman) studied law. One of the Beecher's daughters married Henry Stanbery, and the other Philadelphus Van Trump, both of whom became distinguished citizens of Lancaster. Two other fine houses, also since destroyed, were the homes of the Rev. John Wright (where the Elks Club now stands) and that of Judge Wm. Irvin, a native of Virginia. Irvin's fine Federal house facing the Public Square was described as the center of "culture and fashion" of Lancaster.

Still standing are several other early brick homes. One is known as the Matlack house, built about 1807 to house servants for a large home later torn down when the elegant Wm. Reese home was built in 1836. Interesting features of this early Matlack house are the twelve over eight hand blown window panes and primitive fireplace, with wooden sink beside it. Remnants of the original green paint of the woodwork may still be seen on the stairway partition.

On the south side of Main Street, facing High Street, there is another brick house supposedly built about 1806 for a Mr. Giani. Here, in 1817, the first Catholic services were held by Father Fenwick, an early missionary from Maryland to the scattered settlements of Ohio and Kentucky. This small house now forms the rear section of the 1824 Mumaugh house.

An 1806 house built for Mr. Giani.

This 1806 brick farm house (now incorporated as a family room in the 1820 Federal house) shows the very large cooking fireplace furnished with many early iron vessels and implements – all Fairfield County pieces.

Near Lancaster, several brick farm houses were built in the early 1800's. One constructed for Mr. Samuel Bush has an exceptionally large cooking fireplace with a narrow steep stairway to the sleeping room above. This early house is now incorporated as the family room of an 1820 Federal farmhouse and has been restored and furnished with many beautiful and rare early utensils from Fairfield County. This fireplace is the earliest cooking fireplace still in use in the county.

Another early brick farmhouse just north of town was built about 1809 for Daniel Arnold. In 1800 Arnold came from Hagerstown, Maryland to this location where he farmed for 30 years. His father, Frederick Arnold, a counterpane weaver, and his four sisters joined him shortly afterwards. In 1810, a brother, Henry Arnold, a successful merchant in Hagerstown, also moved his family to Lancaster, where he purchased property and commenced a dry goods business.

Two miles north of Lancaster Daniel Arnold built this fine regional Federal farmhouse for his family, in 1809. They had come from Maryland. The 12/12 windows, fine woodwork detail and stairway, kitchen in the ground floor with its large cooking fireplace were very commodious at that time. The porch was a later addition.

In 1810, a frame market house was constructed on the south west corner of Zane's Square. Above was built the first Masonic Temple. The Palladian windows again exhibit the interest held by the first builders in classic design. Here Charles Sherman organized the first Grand Commandery of Ohio.

About the same time, 1810, a frame market house with a room above for the use of the Masons, was built on the southwest part of the Public Square. In this building the first Grand Commandery of Ohio was organized. The lovely Paladian window in the Masonic room shows the earliest builders' interest in Federal architecture.

Charles Robert Sherman was the son and grandson of prominent judges in Connecticut, and as such was destined for the bar. Following his graduation from Dartmouth College, he studied law in his father's office, in 1810 was admitted to the bar, and married Mary Hoyt, a childhood friend from a prominent family, who had also recently graduated from the fashionable M.E. & A. Sketchley's Seminary in Poughkeepsie. Sherman soon headed west alone to find his father's Revolutionary acres, where he hoped to build a house and start the practice of law . . . "The Indians, however, changed his plans for as late as 1810 northern Ohio, where his father's grant was located, was still dangerous territory. So Charles Sherman came to Lancaster, whose unusual civilization in the wilderness delighted him" . . . He opened a law office and became convinced that this new town was promising enough that it must become his home. He returned to Connecticut and the following Spring, with his gently bred wife and newborn son, made the return trip by horseback, over the near thousand mile trail through the wilderness to their new home, a two-story frame house on Main Street, halfway up the hill.

Soon Charles Sherman became a prominent member of the community, being appointed county attorney. With the coming of the War of 1812, he was elected major and chief recruiting agent for the Fourth Regiment of Ohio Militia. Although only twenty-four years of age, he had become the chief patriotic speech maker of the region. Like all settlers in the northwest, Sherman heard much about the Indian leader Tecumseh whose bravery, humanity, and statesmanship was looked upon with admiration by all thoughtful settlers. When peace came to the nation, Sherman went back to the practice of law and success – but vowed a son of his should be named for the brave, diplomatic, and merciful Indian Tecumseh.

Charles Sherman was one of the first trustees of the new Ohio University and in May 1815 examined and awarded Thomas Ewing the first Bachelor of Arts degree to be awarded in the Northwest Territory. It was inevitable that young Ewing decided to come to Lancaster to study law, for he so admired Charles Sherman, and considered Lancaster both progressive and cultured.

Sherman's family grew yearly, but it was not

until 1820 that a red-haired son was born whom he could name Tecumseh. In 1813 Charles Sherman had been appointed Collector of Internal Revenue by President Madison and thus was responsible for the collection of taxes in six counties, where he had deputies. Most taxes were paid by local bank notes which in 1817 the U.S. Government suddenly refused to accept. Refusing to desert his deputies, Sherman mortgaged his home and most of his future earnings to work off the indebtedness, thus becoming impoverished for years – but his reputation for integrity and deep friendships with men of consequence across the whole state long outlived him. His home was referred to in the newspapers as "the center of refined hospitality" a description probably accurate since in all of Lancaster there was no other couple with the social and educational background of the Shermans. Prominent visitors such as Governor DeWitt Clinton, Henry Clay, and the elegant Duke of Saxe-Weimar made the simple Sherman home their headquarters.

In 1823 Sherman was elected a judge of the Ohio Supreme Court and served until 1829 when he suddenly took ill, in Lebanon, Ohio, while holding court, and died leaving the gentle Mary Hoyt Sherman with eleven children to rear!

This pencil sketch shows the simple frame home built by Charles Sherman. In 1811, it was but a four room cottage with a lean-to kitchen. Then in 1816, as his family grew, several additional rooms were added.

Restored by the Fairfield Heritage Association, this room depicts the dining room in the 1811 section. Though simply furnished, this home radiated the "refined hospitality" for which the Shermans were famous. All of the Sherman's eleven children became successful and prominent citizens, but two of them, US Senator John Sherman (famed for the Anti-Trust Act) and General William Tecumseh Sherman, achieved national prominence, thus their birth place and early home is listed as a National Landmark. (See page 142, <u>Sherman House</u>).

Examples of early pottery and a wooden bowl, made from a maple burl, locally made for household use.

From the beginning mechanics and craftsmen were encouraged to settle in New Lancaster, for furniture, clothing and every conceivable thing was made by hand. There were good chair makers, wheelwrights, gunsmiths, carpenters, blacksmiths, shoe makers, tailors, hat makers, weavers, harness makers, plow makers, wagon makers, rope makers, tanners, tinners and coppersmiths, and many of their descendants still live here and cherish early examples of their workmanship. There were also silversmiths, as well as ministers, lawyers, and doctors. Only a few of these skilled craftsmen signed their work – most of the identifiable pieces have simply descended in the families.

Fancy stenciled chair-locally made and decorated.

Walnut cradle made for and used in the home of Dr. Simon Hyde.

Made at Bope's Corner, this early dry sink is unusual because of its decorative back board, a primitive craftsman's attempt to recreate the ever-popular sunburst.

Early plank bottom chair with curved arrow back spindles.

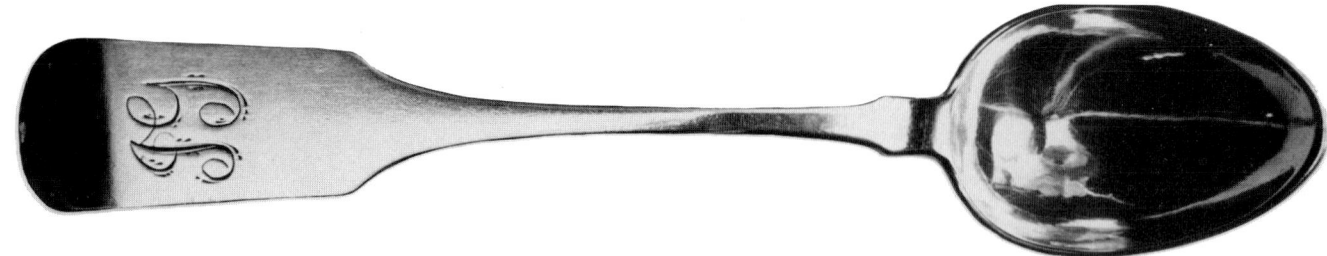

Coin silver spoon made for Mrs. Ruhama Green, one of the earliest settlers, by silversmith T. Sturgeon.

Face of one of the many clocks locally assembled in the shop of Timothy Sturgeon and his son Thomas, silversmiths.

Timothy Sturgeon, who came to Lancaster in 1800 from Dauphin Co., Pennsylvania, was a silversmith and clock maker. He is one of the few who signed his work. His shop and house were located just east of the Public Square, on what came to be known as "Sturgeon's Row". His son Thomas carried on the business with his father.

Very little of the early coin silver was marked. However, one coin silver spoon is stamped "T.S." and was known to have been made in the Sturgeon Shop for Mrs. Ruhama Green, wife of John Green, one of the aforementioned first settlers. She had previously survived capture by the Indians, at which time her first husband, Charles Bilderback, had been scalped! The spoon is now the property of a local descendant.

There are more surviving clocks having the signatures of either Tim Sturgeon, T. Sturgeon or Thomas Sturgeon than there are silver pieces. It is believed that the works for the clocks were obtained in England, the tall cases made by local cabinet makers and assembled and marked by the Sturgeons. The fact that all the known clocks are still in good running order is a testimonial to their skill. In style the clocks range from the finest inlaid Hepplewhite to the then popular Empire.

This clock marked "Thos. Sturgeon, Lancaster, Ohio," had descended from early days in one family until the last one died. This clock is entirely original – no refinishing.
While each of these clocks is different, most have similar characteristics.

This clock, marked "Tim, Sturgeon, Lancaster, Ohio," has descended in the Work Family – currently owned by Edgar Work. Timothy Sturgeon and John Work both served on the June Grand Jury of Fairfield County, in 1806. Timothy Sturgeon died in 1826. Because of the rope carving some feel that this clock must have been made late in his career. Because of the height of the clock, at some time the finials were removed from it.

But there are other locally made, unsigned, clocks which have descended in local families. While most are made of cherry, one, of tiger striped maple, is the work of a talented early local cabinet maker.

Barter was often used, and one cabinet maker, Isaiah Vorys, Sr., who made a cherry tall case for himself, used this system to obtain the works and face for his clock. He made and traded a coffin for the clock works!

Among the early mechanics, George Sanderson, Edward Shaeffer, Jacob D. Dietrick and John Hermann were printers and publishers. Sanderson's paper was the "Independent", which he abandoned to go to the War of 1812.

Feeling against Great Britain ran high and Sanderson raised a company, was elected captain, and marched to the Northwest to join General Hull at Detroit, who almost immediately surrendered them to the British. Disgusted with Hull's conduct, Sanderson broke his sword over a stump rather than turn it over to the British. Paroled, he returned home to raise another company to join General Harrison in the fight. Never known to have fear, George Sanderson was the boy of 12 years who carried the mail through the wilderness.

After the victory, he returned to Lancaster a hero, was elected to the Legislature for several terms, and then founded the *Lancaster Gazette*.

As early as 1809 Shaeffer and Dietrick published the "Ohio Eagle" in both German and English because there were so many German speaking residents. In 1817 John Hermann became editor of the *Eagle* and *Der Deutsche Ohio Adler*.

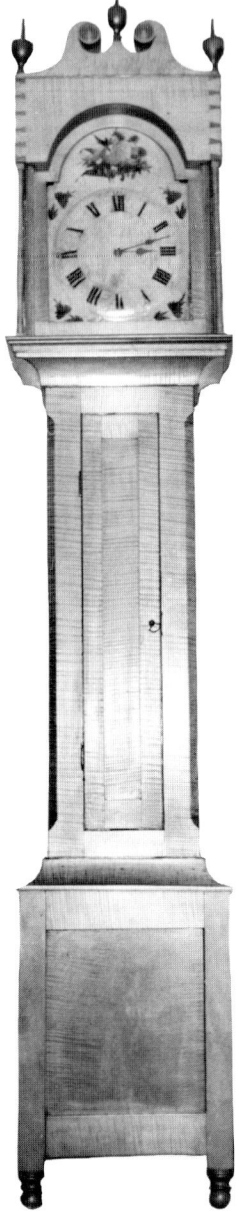

This unmarked clock of tiger striped maple has descended many generations in the family of the original owner.

Very rare colored wax silhouettes of John Hermann and his wife – probably made in Philadelphia, but artist unknown.

A typical Pennsylvania Dutch fractur made by F. Krebs for Christian Gramlich (later angelicized to Crumley) in 1802.

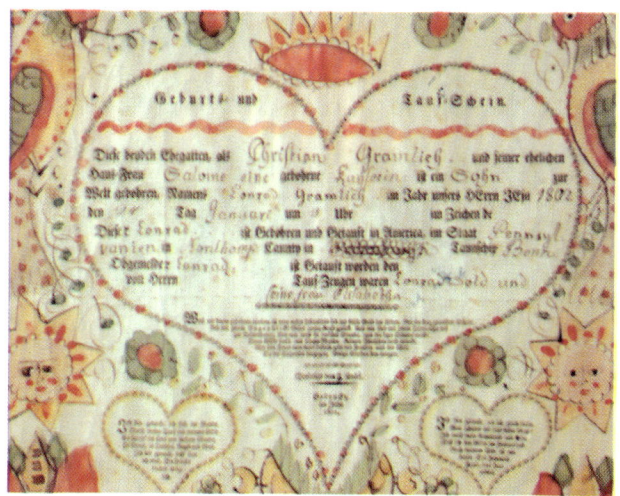

Hand made Pennsylvania Dutch fractur (birth certificate) of Magdalena Toellerin, born January 3, 1805, showing in the red, white and blue shields, the patriotic fervor of the earliest settlers. She later married Conrad Crumley.

Another interesting colorful certificate of Joseph Kemmerer was issued March 15, 1820 in Fairfield County, Ohio – North America. It had been printed in Lancaster, Ohio in 1817 by John Hermann.

This birth certificate of Samuel Effinger (one of Lancaster's most prominent early citizens, a successful tin and coppersmith who built one of the finest early Federal houses where Shaw's Inn now stands) says he was born in Millerstown, Shenandoah County, Virginia on July 18, 1792. He came to Lancaster in 1813.

This painted wooden chest with decorative iron bands probably accompanied German immigrants when they came to this country in 1724 and several generations later was brought to the Ohio country from Pennsylvania.

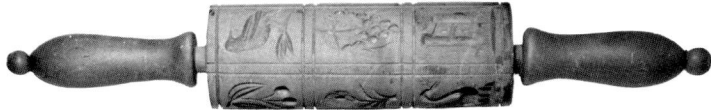

Several different kinds of wooden cookie moulds used by the thrifty and often artistic Pennsylvania Dutch hausfrau.

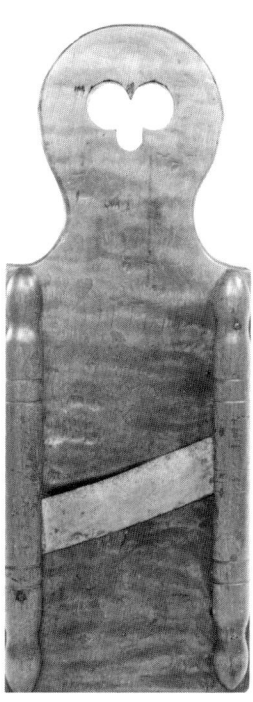

A preponderance of the earliest settlers were so called "Pennsylvania Dutch" who came here from Eastern Pennsylvania. Many of their ancestors had come from Germany and Switzerland, settling in Pennsylvania before the Revolution. With them as they travelled west to Ohio they brought their birth certificates, some cherished pieces of furniture and their skills and habits of industry and thrift. The county seat of Fairfield County, Ohio, was named New Lancaster because the Carpenter family and so many others came from, in or near Lancaster, Pennsylvania.

Decorated sauerkraut cutter, also used by early hausfrau.

31

Mayer – Marquette – Morrow

In 1807 David Mayer received from Thomas Jefferson his land grant for a large farm in Berne Township. A few years later, he built this sandstone house, the only known stonehouse in Fairfield County. A simple four room cottage, originally, with cherry floor boards 20" wide, it has been restored.

Nearby, on a hillside location is a double-pen, or saddlebag, log barn, allegedly built by Wyandot Indians. The foundation and first level of the barn is of the same large sandstones as the house. It has interesting barred windows.

Because of difficult and slow travel, there were many early taverns along Zane's Trace and in Lancaster, but all traces of most of them are gone.

In "New" Lancaster, Samuel Graybill presided over a fine big *Green Tree Tavern*, and . . . "set great store by his marvelous sign, which some do say he painted. In an elaborate, carved frame the panel depicted Mine Host on horseback, in red coat, riding to the hounds, while up a tree crouched a fox 'Sly Fellow'. The Green Tree was a very fashionable place! . . ."

There were also the graceful *Golden Swan* and the *Golden Sun*.

In West Rushville there still stands a brick house, once a tavern. Here in West Rushville, as the temperance movement gained momentum, Rufus Putnam advertised at his tavern bar "Ice Cream, Soda, Hot Coffee, etc. would be kept constantly on hand for the temperate." But a nearby competitor, Amos G. Bright, proprietor of *The Lafayette, Sign of the American Coat of Arms* replies "To the Temperate! He is so unfortunate as not to be able to hold out any inducements, having neither ice cream or soda."

Only known remaining early tavern in Fairfield County probably built about 1810. Located in West Rushville along Zane's Trace, its large sandstone foundation blocks and entrance way, and its brick construction have made it more impervious to the ravages of time than the many earlier log taverns along the Trace.

Adam mantel in the spacious living room of the above Tavern. There are good mantels in each room, as that was the only method for heating. In the kitchen is a large cooking fireplace.

In Lancaster, Colonel John Noble, who came from Maryland about 1815, owned and operated The Union Hail, the first weather boarded log tavern. It burned to the ground, but Noble replaced it with a fine brick structure called the Phoenix, the sign displaying a... "Resplendent Phoenix Bird arising from the flames". Here he entertained many important guests – Henry Clay, James G. Blaine when running for President and Governor DeWitt Clinton of New York. All that is left of Noble's early Tavern is this ink stand showing the same Phoenix arising from the flames. Colonel Noble later moved to Columbus and established the Neil House.

1815 – 1840
Era of Classic Revival Building
Georgian – Federal – Greek Revival

The conclusion of the War of 1812-14, which had been supported in Fairfield county by several hundred young volunteers, under the leadership of George Sanderson, John Williamson and John Leist, brought in its aftermath the "Era of Good Feelings" as contemporaries called it. With the fear of both the British and the Indians finally subdued, patriotism and pride of country were everywhere evidenced. Here in Fairfield County permanent institutions were being founded, and fine permanent homes were being planned and built. The population soon doubled and the need for good craftsmen and mechanics was great, and fortunately many came.

Daniel Baker, Wm. Duffield, James Hampson, Joshua Clark, Henry Miers, James Weakley, Isaac Church, Christopher Weaver, Isaiah Vorys, Sr. and Henry Orman were among the earliest carpenters. All were "well read" in architectural subjects. Wm. Cassell was noted for designing and building fine stairways. There were also good cabinet makers, stone masons, brick makers, plasterers, wood carvers and iron workers. Few signed their work, and not too many records are available; therefore, it is difficult to attribute, in many cases, just who was responsible for a particular fine piece of workmanship.

Coming as they did in both directions over Zane's Trace, and probably trained in their respective trades in Eastern Pennsylvania, Kentucky, Maryland or Virginia, with some coming directly from Germany, these master craftsmen also had available to them Asher Benjamin's and other handbooks. These they freely used to construct beautiful mantels, doorways, arches and stairways. Therefore, we find in Lancaster and Fairfield County an interesting mixture of many architectural influences – Southern, Philadelphia, New England – all adapted to this location and often, because of a fifty year lag behind

Watercolor of an early gentleman carrying his high beaver hat. As early as 1817, the Ohio Eagle was carrying advertisements for hats made to order, and for dressmakers who had the latest fashions and materials from New York!

their eastern counterparts, showing a transition between styles: thus, a Greek temple style with Gothic windows!

Soon the prominent citizens were erecting fine houses, befitting their status – and there were many excellent craftsmen equal to the task of building such houses, and cabinet makers to supply much of the furniture. Sadly, only a few of them left records of their work. The best evidence of their craftsmanship is the structure itself. Much of the fine furniture and artifacts have been removed to every part of the United States, either by descendants or by antique dealers who early scoured this county. Some of which remains here can be identified as being locally made, and some probably was brought with them by early settlers.

The question has often been asked "Why were so many fine homes built in such a small village as Lancaster was at that time?" In 1815 Lancaster's population was about 1,000. In the 1820's the population doubled and there were a number of well educated and enterprising young men who established very successful commercial ventures. The first Medical Society in Ohio was formed here in 1824. The Bar of Lancaster was prominent not only throughout the state of Ohio, but in the nation's Capitol. Good academies were founded early, and by 1830 a public school system and free public library were established.

Businesses of all kinds – newspapers, foundries, banks and stores flourished and the men involved in these enterprises prospered.

Among the earliest builders was John Leist, born in Northhampton County, Pennsylvania in 1774, who had settled in Dutch Hollow, Clear Creek Township in 1807. Coming home from the War of 1812, he was elected to the Ohio Legislature where he served from 1813-1820. Four fine houses which he built still

Portrait of an early Lancaster citizen. Subject and artist unknown.

stand. The excellence of his craftmaship, and his knowledge of Federal architecture, probably gained through keen observation of similar houses in his native state, plus the use of Asher Benjamin's and other Hand Books for American Builders, are all to be observed in these four houses. Handsome proportion, wood carving details and excellent stone and brick masonry are all found in these homes which, at the time, were built in wilderness country. Burning the bricks from local clay, on the site, taking large blocks of sandstone from nearby quarries, and utilizing walnut trees cut down to clear the site was the first part of the operation. But putting them together with knowledge of style and expert craftmanship make these early examples outstanding.

1817 Leist – Veffer

This house, the first and smallest house by John Leist, was built in 1817 – so marked in a small stone in the pediment of the house. The hand hewn timbers, marked with Roman numerals, are put together with wooden pins. The detail of the woodwork is extremely fine, as is the proportion of the delicate spiral stairway. The kitchen has a huge cooking fireplace, with a stone sink beside it (surely a modern convenience in 1817!).

Hand forged shutter dogs of an interesting design hold the shutters of this 1817 home in place.

Graceful spiral stairway, with finely detailed bridge board and woodwork.

Elongated sunburst detail over interior door used first in the 1817 house but later used in all the houses built by John Leist.

Parlor mantel in the 1817 house built by John Leist.

Elaborate cornice and fine cupboards are found in the 1817 dining room.

1820 Leist – Smith

After living in a log cabin for more than ten years, Valentine Reber's wife, neé Magdalena Van Roden, longed for a fine house similar to the house she had left behind in Berks County, Pennsylvania. Reber was the owner of a whole section of land, a prosperous and influential man in the county, so he employed John Leist to build him a handsome house. Much of the same detail found in the 1817 house is also used here, but with more elaboration to fit this larger 1820 house.

Interior of the front door of the 1820 Valentine Reber house. The elliptical fan light, egg and dart moulding, original lock (marked J. Kindler, Lancaster, Ohio – 1826-29) and fine woodwork detailing mark this house as the work of fine craftmanship.

(1820) Detail of stylized wheat carving to embellish the window frames of the parlor.

All of John Leist's houses have similar fine detailing. This elongated sunburst is almost his trademark, as it is to be found in all of his houses.

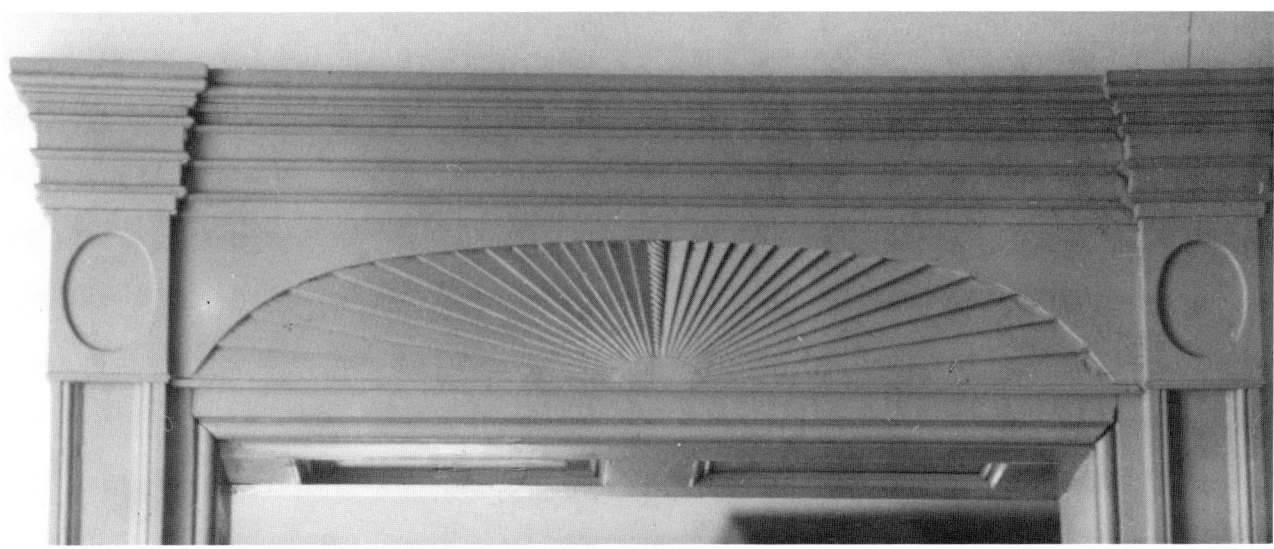

The detail of reeded columns and graceful curves of the stair rail and dado are unusual for a country home of this period.

The sunburst motif is again used with double reeded columns and Ionic capitals on another mantel.

Adam influence is reflected by the hand carved urns of this mantel, which also exhibits the ever popular sunburst.

1824 Leist – Mathias – Strausbaugh

The large 1824 house, was "modernized" or Victorianized by the addition of a bracketed cornice, but the handsome doorway and some of the same woodwork detail mark it as a Leist house also.

Stone door casing surrounds the original fanlight and a replaced door in this country home built by John Leist in 1824.

1827 Leist – Cluff – Weinberg

Finally in 1827, John Leist built for himself, at Dutch Hollow, another brick house. The unusually fine doorway detail, with rope carving in stone on the exterior frame and the same rope carving in wood on the interior door frame, the elongated sunburst detail over some interior doors, the graduated detail of the stair bridge board, the interesting carved mantels mark all of these country homes as very sophisticated indeed for their time and location.

Also of sandstone, quarried not far behind the house, are huge foundation stones and interesting fence posts.

For his own home, John Leist, in 1827, put an Adam design stone casing, similar to the 1820 house, around his front door but embellished it further with rope carving.

He erected around his home a fence having these interesting carved stone fence posts at strategic points.

1824 Ewing – Kirn – Ryckman

The reeded, free standing columns with Ionic capitals flank the handsome doors and windows of the 1820 parlor of the Thomas Ewing house.

Built for Thomas Ewing at the top of Main Hill, this handsome Federal house has a fine doorway with elliptical fanlight, a matching palladian window above and a semi-circular window in the pediment. The sandstone wall and interesting entranceway from the sidewalk add to the importance of the house.

The interior of the house has especially fine woodwork with free standing Ionic columnettes at the doorway and windows of the parlor, a beautiful archway and mantel in the dining room, and fine stairway.

Thomas Ewing, the first graduate of Ohio University in 1815, became an eminent lawyer, orator and Whig politician. He was twice elected to the U.S. Senate, in 1831 and 1851. In 1841 he was the Secretary of the Treasury in President Harrison's cabinet and in 1849 he became the *first* Secretary of the Interior, under President Taylor, and organized that department. He was a frequent advisor to President Lincoln.

1834 Reese – Peters

William J. Reese was born and educated in Philadelphia. As a young lawyer, he came to Lancaster in 1827 and began to practice his profession. He was a cultured, refined and brilliant young man and soon became one of Lancaster's most prominent citizens. In 1829 he married Mary Elizabeth Sherman, oldest daughter of Charles and Mary Sherman, and they built this handsome Philadelphia type Federal house next door to the Sherman's modest home.

Its fine proportions and imposing location standing high above the street, with the sandstone dry masonry retaining wall, has long excited the admiration of artists. The front portico, with its composite Corinthian columns has 80 beautifully hand carved acanthus leaves. On the side porch the columns are Egyptian inspired Corinthian columns (lotus) and at the rear of the house the columns are simple Doric.

In 1994 the house was donated by the Peters Family for use by the public as an arts/education center.

Hand carved woodwork in drawing room, thought to have been carved in Philadelphia by a pupil of Wm. Savery, and brought over the mountains in covered wagons to be installed in this house.

Detail of hand carved acanthus leaves used to form Corinthian columns.

Unusual square plaster work on ceiling of main hall. Talbot Hamlin, architectural historian, stated that this was the only square ceiling piece he had seen.

Unsupported spiral staircase to third floor, designed by William Cassell

Traveling writing desk.

This Grand Harmonicum, a rare musical instrument, was one of the prized possessions brought over the mountains in 1836 by David and Rebecca Kutz from their Carlisle, Pennsylvania, home. It is a beautiful cabinet holding glasses of various sizes, which hold varying quantities of water. It is played by rubbing dampened fingers along the edges of the glasses, producing bell-like tones. During the rough wagon trip, six of the glasses were broken. Now obsolete, this instrument was invented by an Austrian, but later improved in Baltimore in 1826. This particular instrument graced the drawing rooms of the Kutz's and their descendents and provided accompaniments for many a gentle musical occasion in Lancaster.

"Fancy" chair, one of a set of four painted for the Fromlet family perhaps by John B. Reed, who as early as 1817 advertised as a sign and chair painter, and who was described as being "of artistic merit, no mean artist for his opportunities" . . .

Especially good early bowed Heppelwhite buffet with inlay, (made locally). Early knife boxes for storing silver.

Gold leaf pier mirror, originally in the Mumaugh house, now in main hall.

Gold leaf mirror over marble mantel in double drawing room. Reputed to have been imported from Italy when the house was built.

Early Silhouette of Samuel Effinger. This was done by a famous silhouettist named Hunnewill, who had no arms so did his cutting with his toes.

1823 Effinger

The Effinger house, which stood where the Shaw's Inn now stands, was built in 1823 by Samuel Effinger. He was a Virginian who had become very successful here in the tinning and coppersmith business. Built in front of an old stage coach tavern, which was retained for use as a service wing, the Federal type house was notable for its excellent doorway and Palladian window above, with stone casing, (keystone has a carved dove) well designed side lights and elliptical fan lights of unusual beauty. The stepped gables were another interesting feature.

Paper dolls – purchased in Lima, Peru by Edward Effinger in 1848 when enroute to California around Cape Horn – and sent to his niece Tella Effinger. Printed in Paris, they depict, in beautiful colors, the luxury costumes of a young lady of fashion of that period.

A fine four drawer chest carries the label of Elisha Tucker, Boston and originally was in the Effinger House – now in the Georgian.

Handsome magenta and gold porcelain jar used in Dr. Michael Effinger's office to hold live leeches. The leeches were used by early doctors to treat infections! The lid of the jar has holes in it to permit the flow of air.

One of a pair of handsome, gold and cobalt blue Sevres vases, originally in the Effinger house.

1824 Garaghty – Mumaugh

In 1824, Michael Garaghty, a native of Ireland who had come to Lancaster in 1804, had been a paymaster to Colonel Williamson's regiment in the War of 1812 and had returned to become the cashier of the first Lancaster Bank, and to build this fine Federal home. The stepped gables probably reflect the Dutch background of the builder, Isaiah Vorys, Sr. The house also boasts a beautiful doorway with elliptical fan light, finely detailed woodwork, and a hand carved mantel. It is known that Vorys had Asher Benjamin's Handbook to use as a guide.

Given to the city by Mrs. Fannie Mumaugh, the house is now used as a center for women's clubs and related activities.

Detail view of the front doorway at the Mumaugh house.

Detail of the hand carving on the Mumaugh living room mantel.

1840
Cox – Hunter – Welsh

This Classic Revival house was built around, and incorporated the original 1803 log house built by Tunis Cox. About 1840 John Hunter, son of Hocking Hunter, built this handsome house for his bride, Mary Duncan of Newark, Ohio. The beautiful facade, with its tall columns was similar to her home in Newark. The curved window frames were duplicated in the design of the iron fence and entrance steps to make an unusually pleasant and harmonious whole.

For a few years this was the home of Richard Outcault, the originator of the comic strips, *Yellow Kid, Buster Brown,* etc. It had been the family home of his wife, Mary Jane Martin. It is of interest to note that his two most famous characters, Buster Brown and Mary Jane, with their dog Tige, were modeled from his two children and their pet dog.

Original drawing by Richard Outcault for one of his famous comic strips.

When Richard Outcault, as a young man, taught art in Lancaster, he painted this picture of Billy, a favorite horse.

1834 Stanbery – Rising

This house was built for Henry Stanbery, law partner of Thomas Ewing. Stanbery was the first Attorney General of the State of Ohio, organizing that department. He later became U.S. Attorney General under President Andrew Johnson. He resigned that office to help successfully defend President Johnson in his impeachment trial. (The house was sold to Philemon Ewing). In 1884, when Philemon Ewing lived in his house, he entertained his cousin, James G. Blaine, who was running for President of the United States.

Here again we see a beautiful Georgian-Federal House. The hand carved cornice on the exterior of the house has long excited architects and artists. It is said to be similar to and perhaps inspired by a similar cornice by Inigo Jones on the Queens House in Greenwich, England. Certainly there are few others.

This stately home was restored in the 1930's by Mr. and Mrs. Russell Rising. Inside is another beautiful stairway, lovely arches, plaster work, mantels and many features of a fine Georgian house.

It is now owned by the First Methodist Church and used as an Education Building.

Excellent craftsmanship is evident in all the fine houses of this period, but this hand carved cornice detail (said to have been inspired by a similar one by Inigo Jones in Greenwich, England) is particularly handsome.

Plaster ceiling decorations were frequently used.

The Greek Key is again used to adorn one of the mantels. The same Greek Key from Asher Benjamin's Handbook is also used on a mantel in the Creed home.

Inside, the woodwork detail is varied and handsome. The corner block motifs seen here, the Greek Key and stylized leaves are from Asher Benjamin's Handbook.

1832 The Georgian

The regency curves and five Ionic fluted pillars, which adorn the portico on the west side of the Georgian, are here shown. From here Samuel F. Maccracken reviewed the various military companies of his day, and to this day crowds gather here to watch Fourth of July and other parades!

In 1830 Samuel Finley Maccracken, (who had come to Lancaster from eastern Pennsylvania as early as 1810 and had become a prominent and successful businessman) employed Daniel Sifford to construct for him a fine house in the center of Lancaster. The beautifully proportioned structure, of modified Georgian design, has some Regency features and was probably inspired by fine examples Maccracken had observed in Philadelphia.

Handsome empire chair, one of a set probably made by J. Woltz of Lancaster, and originally used in the Georgian.

The five column portico on the west side is thought to have been a dramatic addition to the original plan, probably added before the house was completely finished in 1832. The two-story, fluted Ionic columns are built around original forest trees of the same height. When they were examined during restoration a man's black high hat was found inside one of the columns!

The thirteen room house is entered through an enormous hall, at the rear of which is a splendid, unsupported, spiral stairway, designed by Wm. Cassel. This leads up three flights of stairs to a skylight in the roof of the central gable. Access to the portico is through $9^1/2$ foot curved window-doors. The large handsome doors between the double parlors are of cherry, with panels of Santo Domingo mahogany. A most unusual matching pair of King of Prussia grey marble mantels is also found here. Restored in the 1970's by the Fairfield Heritage Association, as a living museum for Fairfield County, it now houses some furniture and artifacts from both the Maccracken and Martin families, and other early Fairfield County pieces which are gifts from descendants of early settlers.

The Georgian is open to the public every afternoon except Monday, though closed during the months of January, February and March. It is also available for special events.

The dining room is furnished with two early Lancaster buffets, banquet table and silver. The cut glass punch bowl belonged originally to the John D. Martins, the second family to own the Georgian.

A glimpse of one of the parlors – with fine early furniture and portraits.

The guest bedroom furnished in the Regency style: bed with pineapple finials and drapery, fine early sewing table, and handsome eglomise gilt mirror.

Through the hallway arch with Ionic columns and egg and dart detail can be seen the spiral stairway to the third floor of the Georgian.

Dramatic view looking up the circular stairway at the Georgian to the lantern above.

Handsome mantel in the regency bedroom of The Georgian. A pair of Argand lamps and a Lancaster-made convex mirror lights and reflects the room.

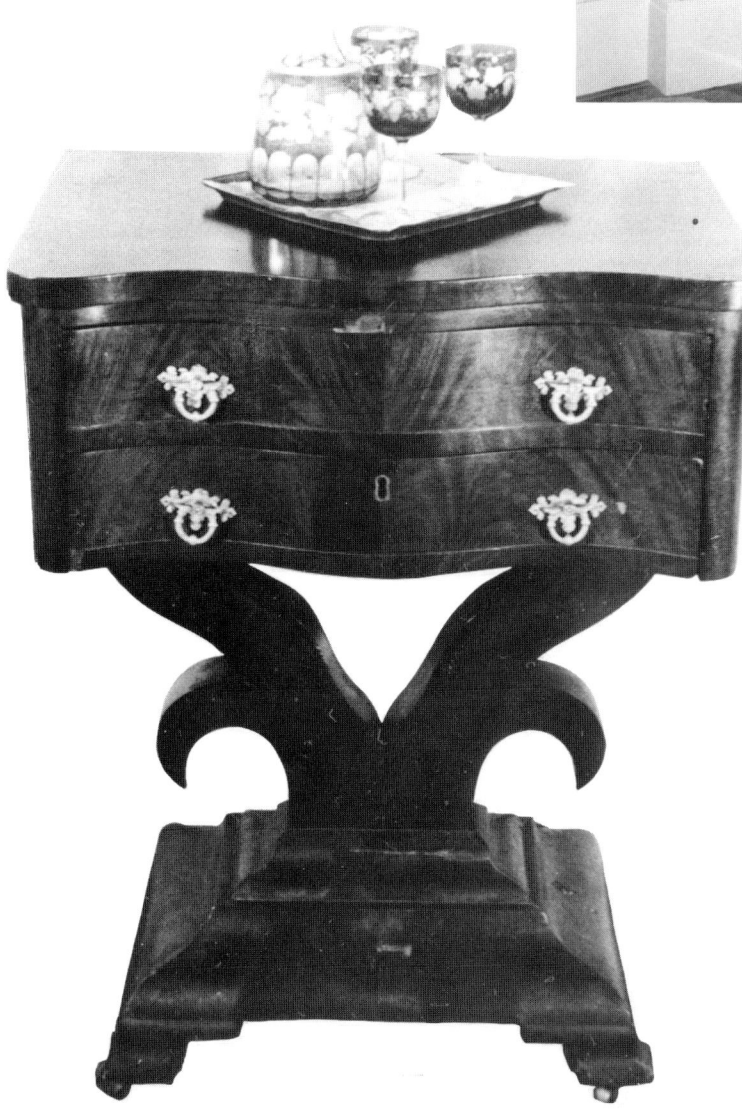

Two drawer serpentine empire cherry stand was originally in the Georgian. The decanter and wine glasses of Bohemian glass also belonged to Sarah and Samuel Maccracken.

Fine tea and coffee service made by T. Whartenby, silversmith in Philadelphia from 1811-1825; given to his bride Sarah Croft Maccracken by Samuel F. Maccracken and used in the Georgian by them.

This elaborate gilt clock, displaying Venus and Psyche, was purchased in Paris and was part of the original furnishings of the Georgian.

Early Lancaster buffet, originally in the John Baldwin House (popularly called the Haunted House). Early coin silver and other silver from the Effinger home.

Table in the kitchen set with early pewter milk jug and plates.

Cooking fireplace in the original basement kitchen of the Georgian. Early ladles, waffle iron, toaster, reflecting oven, and various iron kettles used in cooking are shown.

A rare "Boyd bed" ca.1835 – an unusually fine construction by Boyd, a free man of color, whose workshop was in Cincinnati.

Tucker porcelain pitcher (first fine porcelain made in the U.S.), purchased by S. F. Maccracken for his new home.

A high chest of tiger striped maple with walnut inlay and walnut used for the secondary wood was made in the early days in Fairfield County, at Bope's Corners; now in the Georgian.

1840 Reese – Mattox – Rockwood

Built about 1840 and later purchased by Henry Reese, the son of Wm. T. Reese and Elizabeth Sherman Reese, this house is one of Lancaster's finest examples of Greek Revival architecture. The pilasters, the details of the pediment and cornice, the symmetry displayed by the one story wings on each side of the main structure are all typical of the Greek Revival style so popular at that time. The interior has a lovely spiral stairway, and a quite unusual curved door frame and a curved door near the top of the stairs.

Also, one of the finest iron fences in Lancaster graces the front of this house. It is of Chippendale design and its delicacy is unusual.

Many of the iron fences in Lancaster have been attributed to the foundries of Gilbert Devol. This Chippendale design with fleur-de-lis posts is an exceptionally graceful design.

This curved door frame, halfway up the spiral stairway of the Reese-Mattox house, boasts a door that is also curved.

Fairfield County two door cherry corner cupboard with reeded pilasters and small sunburst decoration.

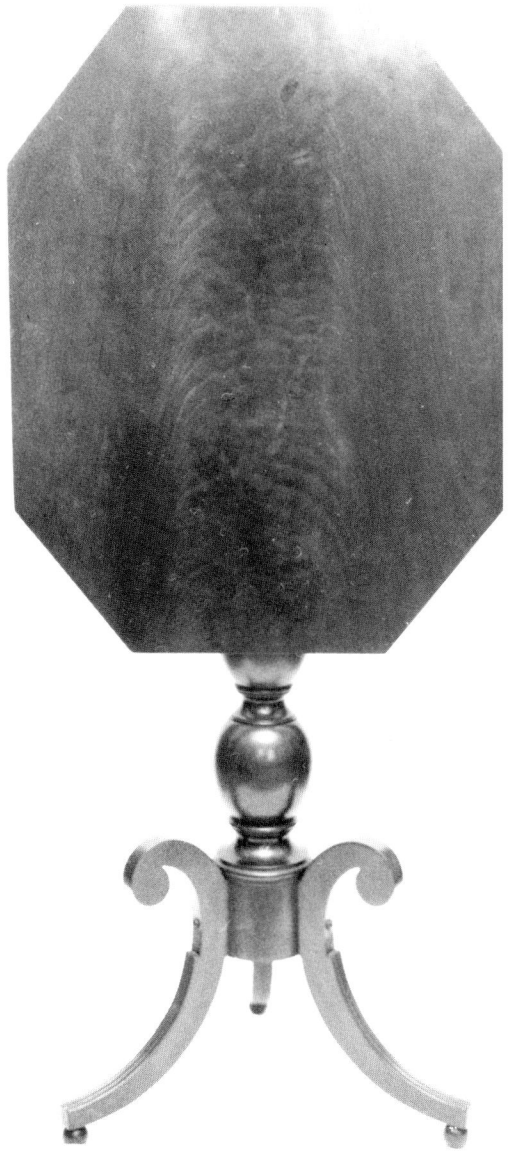

Cherry candlestand made by Isaiah Vorys, Sr.

Two drawer sewing cabinet.

1834 DeVol – Dallow – Anchor Guest House

Across Wheeling Street from the Georgian, Daniel Sifford built another fine Federal house for Joseph Grubb (a portrait and sign painter and chairmaker) who almost immediately sold it to Gilbert DeVol, who had started a very successful foundry and machine shop. (It is of interest to note that DeVol was born in a "blockhouse" of Campus Martius since his father was Capt. Jonathan DeVol, pioneer member of the famous Ohio Company.) It is thought that many of the fine fences in Lancaster were made in his foundry.

The house has a handsome doorway and the woodwork throughout is very beautiful. In 1977 the Anchor Hocking Corporation acquired and restored it as a guest house for official visitors to the corporation.

Fine mantel, with sunburst decoration and double reeded columns, original to the Effinger house, but placed in the DeVol-Dallow home when the Effinger house was dismantled.

The spiral stairway leading to the third floor has an unusual curved doorway near the second floor. (This doorway was moved from the Effinger house at the time it was torn down and placed in this similar position by Mrs. Joseph Dallow)

This handsomely detailed arch in the upstairs hall was also rescued by Mrs. Dallow from the Effinger house.

Beside the mantels in the drawing rooms are built-in gun cases. In the entrance hall there is an Ionic archway, beautiful detailed woodwork throughout with an unusual window-door opening onto a rear terrace and walled garden.

Handsome gun made in Lancaster, signed by George Claspill. He was born in Virginia and described as a silversmith by trade and good at every kind of delicate mechanical work!

1833 Deppe – Heisey

This frame house was built for Julius Deppe, a pioneer doctor, around a two-story log house. The front section, with its graceful stairway and woodwork, was added in 1837 by John B. Reed, artisan. The interesting board and pattern carriage house in the rear, with stalls for six horses, was built about 1870. A lovely little garden is between house and carriage house.

The logs of the 1833 part of the house have been uncovered in the kitchen. Here we also see the narrow steep stairway to the second floor of the log house.

1830 Matlack – Burns – Roche

Thought to have been built by John Matlack, this early brick house has had many owners. In 1859, while her husband, General W. T. Sherman, was assigned to the Louisiana Military Academy, Ellen Ewing Sherman and her children rented the house and lived here for a few years.

Charming two drawer sewing table made of five kinds of wood–maple, cherry, ash, hickory and butternut – by an early Fairfield County cabinet maker.

1833 Ferguson – Furniss – Nolan

New England Federal Architecture describes this rectangular house, which is one of the few early frame structures. It was built of hand split native tulip poplar. Standing beside the house is a giant 150 year old tulip tree which towers over the house and garden. "Bully" Wm. F. Ferguson, one of the first owners, was for many years the Commander of the Lancaster Blues, a stylish militia company which participated in many of the colorful events of the 1830's, including the opening of the Lateral Canal in Lancaster and the laying of the cornerstone of the Capitol in Columbus.

Elaborate gilt chandelier, originally in the Hocking Hunter house.

Entrance to the home Daniel Sifford started about 1845 for himself – but left unfinished to go to California with the gold rush. He later returned but the house was not completed until the 1890's by Mr. A. I. Vorys. Please note the cornice and acanthus trim by the door.

Sifford – Vorys – Wiseman – American Legion

Daniel Sifford, who built so many of Lancaster's fine homes, started this house for himself in the 1840's. About 1852 he went to California, along with others, to find gold. Two years later he returned to Lancaster and continued in the building business. He apparently did not have the funds to complete the house, so lived in it unfinished until his death. In 1890 the house was sold at Sheriff's sale, and purchased by Mr. A. I. Vorys who completed the building, adding a large front porch – which had at that time become fashionable. In 1913, it was sold to the Wiseman family, who owned it until it was purchased for an American Legion Home in the 1930's.

The stone entrance way has unusually fine carving. The main entrance has acanthus carving detail, and there is an attractive spiral stairway.

The rear of the house has a large addition to adapt it to American Legion activities.

A detail of the facade of the Hummel Greek Revival home, circa 1840, showing the Greek Key used as decorative corner blocks on the windows and the lintels of the wide cornice.

Greek Key detail on mantel of Creed house.

Greek key design from Asher Benjamin's Handbooks was frequently used by early local builders in various ways.

Detail of the intricate Greek key design used to embellish an upstairs mantel in the Sifford-Legion home.

Town Cottages of the Classic Era

Clark-Romano-Ridley Cottage

Huddle-Spires Greek Revival Cottage

Schultz – Dumm – Kocher. Early frame cottage, typical of many built in Lancaster by the Pennsylvania Germans.

Sifford – Osterhage – Ogilvie. Early home of Daniel Sifford, one of Lancaster's fine builders.

In the first Methodist church building in Lancaster (now the Masonic Temple) we see the transition from Greek Revival to Gothic Revival. The pediment, cornice, pilasters and belfry show the classic Greek influence, while the pointed windows show the Gothic.

The second Presbyterian church, first used in 1834, was a handsome two story brick structure whose architect was Isaac Church, who settled here in 1816. Mr. J. A. Weakley was the builder. It is of interest that a group of prominent citizens petitioned the Presbyterians to have a clock installed in their tower, but it was never done.

Spook Hollow: Bush – Turner – Gurile/Schwartz

Part of this farm house was built for Samuel Bush as early as 1806. This original cottage with its huge fireplace is now the family room. The brick front was added about 1820, and is in the Federal style. It received its colorful name because of a "spook" which was supposed to have haunted it in the early days.

Plain on the exterior, this house is notable for its fine woodwork, mantels and stairway. Built near a spring of clear water (which still runs) the house is surrounded with many varieties of native plants of great beauty. Restored by Mr. and Mrs. Herbert Turner, it is on the National Register.

Spook Hollow before restoration

Coin silver spoon made in Lancaster by Gates and Casper, Silversmiths.

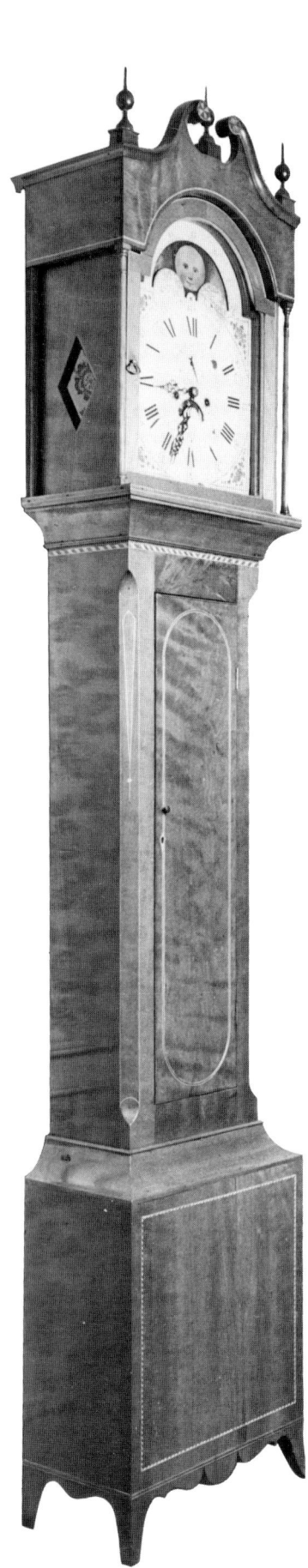

Cherry drop leaf table-made in 1824 by Jesse Woltz– one of the few cabinet makers who signed their work.

Fine Hepplewhite style cherry inlaid clock, attributed to Thomas Sturgeon.

1838 Wilson – Monger

Nathaniel Wilson, one of the earliest settlers in Fairfield County, built this fine Greek Revival home on his large farm in the 1830's. The pilasters, finely detailed cornice and symmetry make his country home outstanding. It is on the National Register.

Detail of Wilson – Monger cornice.

Early lantern carried by Mrs. Nathaniel Wilson

Stonewall Cemetery is noted for being one of the finest examples of dry stone masonry in Ohio.

The inscription above the gate and below the keystone reads as follows:
This wall encloses the family burying ground of Nathaniel Wilson, Sr. (one of the early pioneers of the West who emigrated from Cumberland County Pa. and settled near this place A.D. 1798 when all around was one continual and uninhabited wilderness) was commenced by him A.D. 1838 and finished in the following year by his son, Gustin, the former having suddenly died May 12, 1839.

This octagonal wall was put into place in 1838. The stones were shaped in a near-by quarry and erected in silence by the workmen while Nathaniel Wilson, a devoutly religious man, read to them from the Bible.

Stone Carving

While sandstone was quarried on a small scale in the earliest days in various parts of the county for local construction, it was not until 1832 that Wendell Strentz, a stone mason recently from Germany, opened and operated the first stone quarry on a large scale. Located in the Southeast corner of the original Zane section, it supplied the stone for the fronts and stone columns of the first bank and many Main Street buildings. Stone for the high walls on Main and Wheeling Streets also came from this quarry. There are many examples of excellent stone carving, but who all the craftsmen were is unknown. John Strickler, stonecutter, is the only one who *signed* his work.

A particularly fine example of early stone carving is this garden ornament of "Rebecca at the Well" – artist unknown.

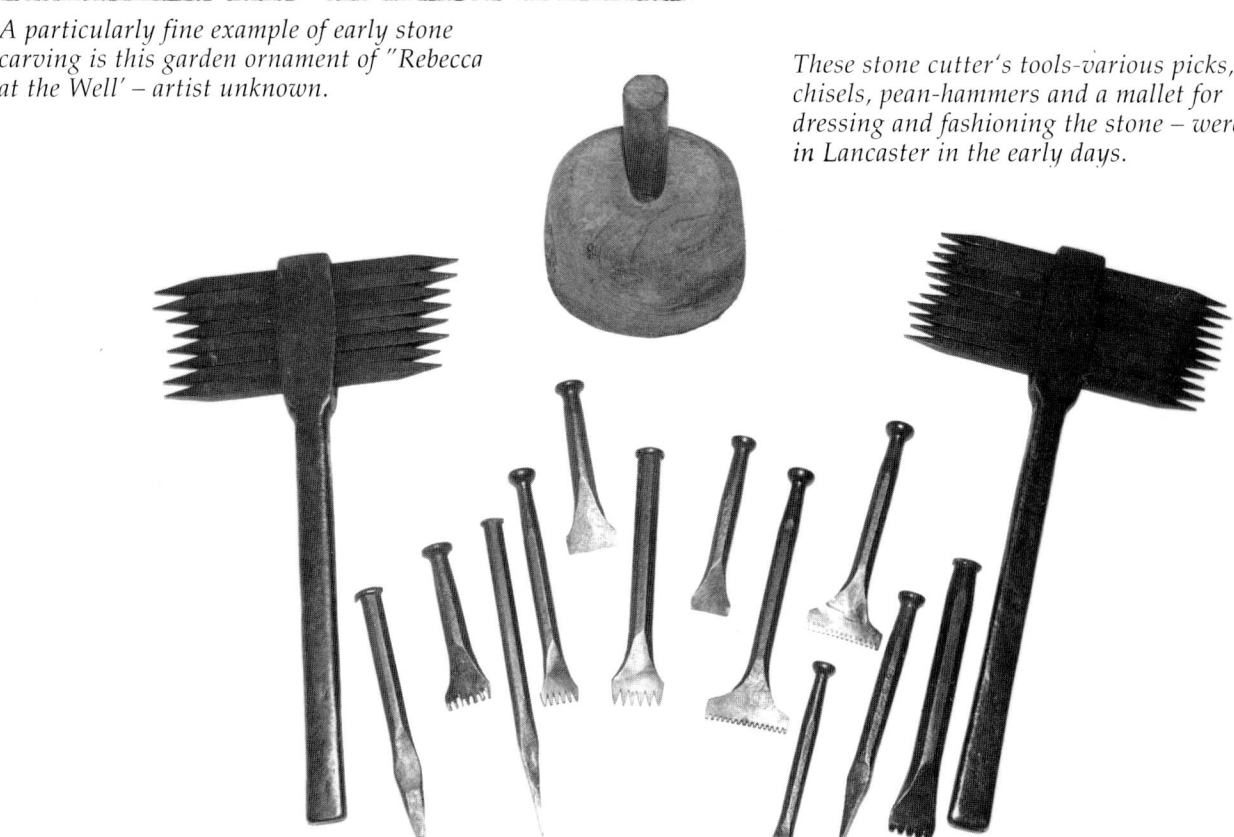

These stone cutter's tools-various picks, chisels, pean-hammers and a mallet for dressing and fashioning the stone – were used in Lancaster in the early days.

Huge sandstone blocks were used in the construction of the locks on the Lateral Canal through the county, built about 1830.

Some of the excellent examples of dry stone masonry wall on Main Hill. There are many soft shades of pink and green with the beige making these sandstone walls objects of beauty.

This fine circular design was cut on the steps and the entrance to the Sifford-American Legion house.

This handsome carved urn is in the keystone of the stone door casing of the home built by Dr. Simon Hyde in Rushville.

In a very early house facing Zane's Trace is found a fine example of moulded brick eaves.

Adam designs carved into the lintels over doors and windows of the early Stout-Adams farm house in south western Fairfield County.

Detail of stone carving in the stone casing of the doorway at Concord Hall.

Several tombstones, dating from 1825 to 1841, cut and signed by John Strickler. They are located in various early small cemeteries. One tombstone notes the deceased was a native of Lancaster County, Old England; all have intricate designs and appropriate verses. On one, an advertisement at the bottom, in phonetic spelling which reads: "John Strickler, Stone Cutter is living One Mile west of the Babtist Meting house at Plesant Run"

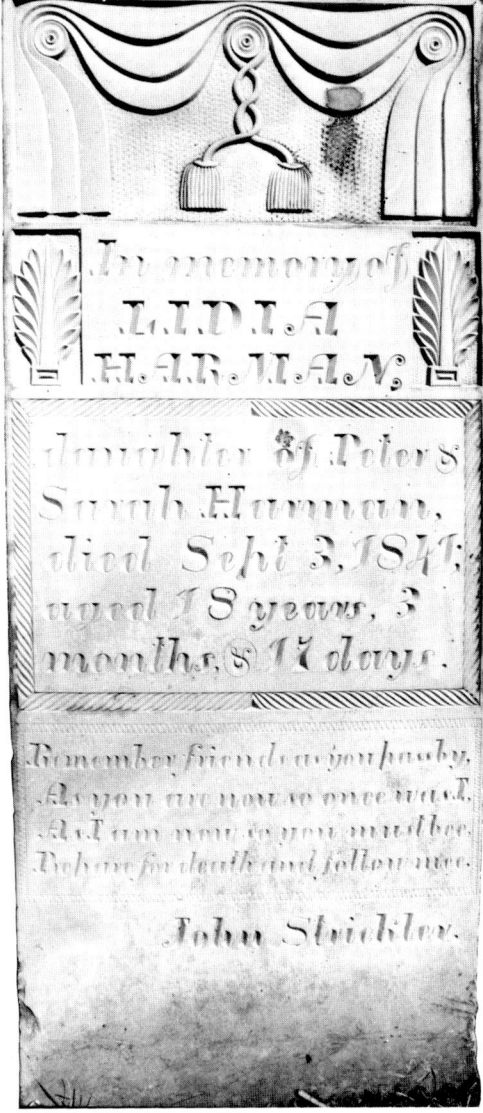

1834 Blair – Brown – Smith

An early Greek Revival home built by Henry Blair who came from Maryland in the early 1830's with Wm. Kincaid. They were stone cutters and carvers. George and Guy Blair carried on the tradition, cutting and carving the stone for St. Mary's Church and the Court House.

A cherry Hepplewhite chest, with excellent proportion, French legs and apron and good strong inlay mark this as the work of a fine early craftsman.

Brumfield-Lanning Greek Revival farm house.

Brumfield – Lanning

Cherry secretary signed by the maker – John Will – 74 years old – 1863.

Very simple three drawer chest, locally made.

The early hillside home of Dr. Van Pearse, while essentially Federal with its lovely stairway and mantels, has been adapted to its location.

Van Pearse – Stuckey

Whitman – Guthrie – Triance

Built for Judge Whitman, this interesting home was the locale for a fictional story in Godey's Ladies Magazine of August, 1862, entitled, "Josie in Mapletown." While the original clapboards have been covered with shingles, many features such as this side porch mark it as one of the good early houses of the Historic District.

Early Furnishings of Fairfield County

Sheraton bow-front chest of drawers with early pink lustre china having handleless cups.

An unusual curly cherry secretary, probably made in Pennsylvania, and brought to Fairfield County in the early 1800's by early settlers in whose family it has descended for many generations.

Early porcelain teapot from the Matlack family, with cup and saucer serving as the lid.

Cherry cannonball four-poster bed, originally belonging to John Creed.

This unusual buffet of burled applewood employs a number of designs. It descended in the family of Samuel Coates, the first postmaster of the Northwest Territory. The maker apparently wanted to use the ever popular sunburst, so he added an inlaid backboard!

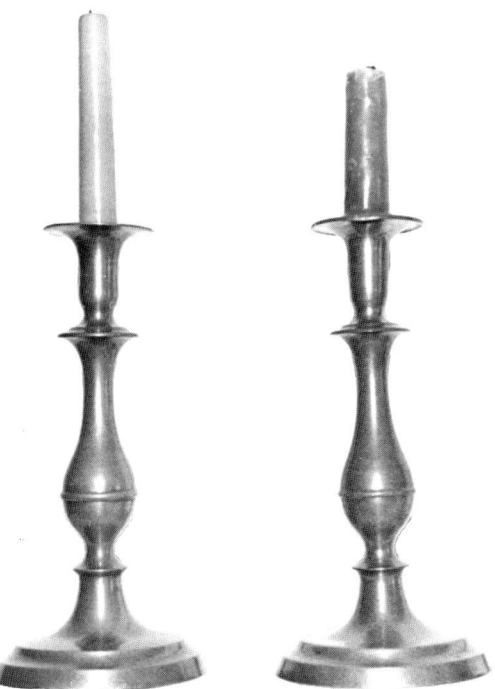

Pewter candlesticks were used in many homes These were made by Sellew and Co., of Cincinnati, Ohio.

Unusual curly maple octagon table made in 1830 by Burrowes Holcombe and brought to Fairfield County.

The works for this early clock were brought from Germany as a wag-on-wall clock. The curly cherry tall case was made by a local unknown cabinet maker.

Delicate reeded four-poster bed which originally belonged to the Thomas Ewing family, now at The Georgian.

In the empire style, with lion's paw feet, this chest of drawers was made in Fairfield County by an unknown cabinet maker. He utilized burled applewood, so popular locally, and trimmed it with bands of tiger striped maple.

Clock of cherry and maple made at Clearport, Ohio.

Two drawer cherry stand, with reeded legs and sandwich glass knobs. It was supposed to have been made in Bremen, Fairfield County.

Pillar and scroll clock by Eli Terry brought into Lancaster.

This fine Sheraton type chest, with unusual carved pilasters, is one of the few signed local pieces. On the back is the signature of Joseph Stepilton, Stoutsville, Fairfield County, Ohio.

Tiger striped maple chest – made by an unknown Millersport cabinet maker.

Concord Hall:

1831 Witte – Fox

In 1829, Captain Augustus Witte emigrated to America and came to Lancaster where he purchased land nearby, erected a steam flour mill and a whiskey distillery and laid the foundation for a fine brick dwelling, the plans for which he had brought from Germany. Then he returned to Germany to bring back his wife and family as well as thirty artisans to help construct his home.

Previously, Captain Witte, a member of a good German family, had received a liberal education and had been on the staff of General Blucher whose niece he had married. He had also participated in the battle of Waterloo.

In 1830, he returned to Fairfield County with his family and lived in a log house while his fine home was being constructed. A fire destroyed the cabin and much of his furnishings, and soon after this event his wife, the former Agatha Von Roden, died leaving five children.

The new dwelling was occupied in 1831, and Captain Witte dispensed hospitality with a lavish hand. The Captain also organized the German Guards, a very finely drilled military company, which participated in the laying of the cornerstone of the State House in Columbus on July 4, 1839.

In 1858, this beautiful farm was sold to John T. Brasee, a prominent lawyer. It is of interest that his daughter Alice, just prior to the Civil War, married George Witte (the son of the first owner) who then lived in New Orleans. She caused a furor at that time by waving a Confederate flag from the "widow's walk" of the house to welcome the bridegroom!

This home is on the National Register.

Fine Victorian gazebo moved from the Stanberry – Rising garden to grace the grounds of Concord Hall.

Carriage house with Victorian detail was built much later than the house.

An unusually elaborate doorway on the second floor of Concord Hall was the entrance to the ballroom.

Portrait of Mrs. Augustus Witte (Agatha Von Roden) with her young daughter, Cecilia. It was painted on copper by an unknown artist in Germany, before they emigrated to this country. Cecilia later married Augustus Mithoff.

Handsome plaster ceiling piece with flowers, grapes, and leaves.

Baker – Love – Smith

In Rushville, many early homes are found. One, built by Dr. Baker, circa 1820, has solid walnut woodwork, spiral stairway, ten working fireplaces. Dr. Baker was active in the underground railway for runaway slaves.

Tombstone recently placed to mark the burial place of Joe Selby, a fugitive slave, who became ill in Rushville, from privations suffered while traversing the underground railway shortly before the Civil War. Dr. Simon Hyde tried to help him, and the Reverend Hanby listened to his plaintive longing for his separated sweetheart Nellie Grey, shortly before he died. Hanby's son, Benjamin wrote the song "Darlng Nellie Grey" to commemorate the pathetic story.

Across the street is the Federal house built by Dr. Simon Hyde. The sandstone door frame is particularly notable, for in the keystone above the elliptical arch is a handsome carved urn. Below it the fan light has the original handblown glass. Ionic receded columns flank the handsome door (which unfortunately is obscured by the aluminum storm door.)

Large red stoneware hand fashioned apple butter jar, glazed on the inside. It originally belonged to Dr. Simon Hyde, of Rushville.

Stout – Mertzger – Perkins

Crites – McDonald

Stenson

Six fine country houses in the classic style, built as soon as possible after their owners were established on their land. Most have walnut woodwork and mantels, but they vary in design and detail.

Bright – Kistler

Davis

Barr

Bope – Franklin

This beautiful doorway is in the fine brick farm house built by Abraham Bope, when all was wilderness. Apparently Bope was a cabinet maker, for we find a number of examples of early furniture which legend has it was made at Bope's Corner. The woodwork shows the fine hand of a master craftsman.

A cherry corner cupboard made at Bope's Corner has sunburst detail on pilasters.

Also made at Bope's Corner, this large four door corner cupboard was constructed of white walnut (or butternut). The cornice and apron are very nice.

1820 The Thomas – Edstrom Farm

Brick house near Tarlton, built in 1820 facing Zane's Trace. It has an ineresting 2nd story porch to the rear and an early smokehouse and springhouse still standing.

Remnant of early stenciled woodwork in the above house. Its stylized trees and leaves in soft shades of blue and green were primitive attempts at home beautification.

Federal type farm house, built in 1830, has interesting woodwork and mantels. Throughout the house the fine hardware and locks were made in England by Carpenter & Co., patented 1825. The nearby springhouse is a Greek Revival structure.

Miller – Beery

Early springhouse, built in Greek Revival style, on the Miller – Beery farm, Where the family probably lived while the large brick house was being built.

Meyer

Waterloo Tavern – built in 1830 near one of the basins for the Ohio-Erie Canal.

Stutzman–Scholl

Stutzman-Scholl brick home, built in 1828, is essentially Federal, adapted to its hillside location which makes it three stories high. Built by an Amish farmer next to a strong spring also used by a nearby Wyandot Indian encampment, this house was the center of the first Amish colony in the county, and was used for their religious services. Great difficulty was encountered, for the sandstone foundation blocks disappeared into quicksand and large white oak logs had to be used as pilings upon which to build the house. The unusual large porch was probably needed to accommodate all the visitors for "meeting". This colony later moved to Holmes County.

Before restoration.

After restoration.

Culp–Kraner–Morgan – Budden

Very early "Virginia" type house in Pleasant Township–now beautifully restored. Built on a small slope, it looks like a one story house in front, but is a full two and a half on the garden side.

111

Country Churches of the Classic Era

This primitive Baptist church can be found at Baptist Corner, near Thurston. The tower displays Victorian features.

St. Paul's Lutheran Church
An early Lutheran church is the second structure built by this congregation. Across the road is the cemetery where there are many interesting early tombstones. Here a number of Wyandot Indians are buried; their graves marked by small boulders with no inscription!

Rushville United Methodist Church
This church, built in 1836 for the Methodist congregation of Rushville, replaced an earlier log structure on the same site. This essentially Federal type, with its interesting belfry and Gothic windows, exhibits the transition in styles which was beginning to occur. The large forged hinges on the door are particularly nice. Daniel Baker, a fine carpenter, came to Rushville from Maryland in 1817, and built this church and most of the good houses in this area.

The Romantic Era
Gothic Revival-Italianate-2nd Empire
1840-1870

The building of the earlier classic and Greek Revival homes had largely expressed admiration for the philosophy of democracy and the patriotic fervor associated with the building of our new nation and the coming of civilization to the frontier. But by the 1840's, a new concept was beginning to take place. Desiring to get away from the formalism of the classic designs, the builders of this period were beginning to reflect the romanticism of the times, and were prolific in their interpretations of the Gothic Revival, the Italianate, and the 2nd Empire styles . . . "What was lost in authenticity was more than made up for in quaintness and uniqueness" . . .

Gothic Revival

Locally, the Italianate style ranges from the Tuscan villa, with its square tower and curved windows, to the basically square house with deep overhanging eaves supported by numerous brackets.

The Gothic Revival style was usually employed for church architecture. A few fine homes of this period display handsome barge boards, and many cottages are embellished with "Carpenter Gothic" decorative detail, combined with pointed windows and arches.

Italianate – Tucscan Villa

The 2nd Empire style was characterized by mansard roofs, with frequent use of iron cresting and dormer windows. All of these styles were mixed, leading to composite effects expressing the builder's individuality. Often an earlier building was modernized by the addition of brackets, towers, and cresting to achieve a picturesque look.

2nd Empire

There was much overlapping of styles, in what is in general known as the Victorian period.

1845 Shaeffer – Voss: Chestnut Ridge

One of the finest examples of Gothic Revival architecture in Fairfield County was built about five miles west of Lancaster by Frederick Shaeffer, an innkeeper in Lancaster "who spent the evening of his days . . . on this fine farm."

On a hill, once in the midst of towering chestnut trees, it commands a fine view of the surrounding countryside.

The exterior is particularly noted for its fine barge board, its original wood porches and unusual tower (an 1890's addition), all of which contrast beautifully with the soft tone of the brick house.

The interior has fine woodwork, in a trefoil design, almost identical to that of St. John's Episcopal Church, which was built by Daniel Sifford.

The original log cabin and an early ice house are still standing. Chestnut Ridge Farm is on the National Register.

The interior woodwork of the Shaeffer-Voss home carries the Gothic treatment in trefoil designs throughout, as does the fine panelling below the windows.

This early photograph of the English Lutheran church, built by Daniel Sifford about 1840, shows the lancet windows and crenelated and pinnacled square tower typical of Gothic Architecture, both medieval and revival.

Since this picture was made the small panes of glass on the windows have been replaced with stained glass windows.

St. John's Church – 1840

English Lutheran Church

This little Gothic Revival church, with its twin crenelated towers and Tudor arch, was inspired by King's Chapel in Windsor, England. Built by Daniel Sifford for the Episcopal Congregation, it is especially noted for its ceiling, which has a motif of white roses on a red field, signifying the union of the House of York with the House of Lancaster, at the conclusion of the War of Roses. C.M.L. Wiseman states in his History of Fairfield County that the red rose is historically the emblematic flower of Lancaster.

Mt. Zion Church – 1890

A country congregation utilized pointed windows, doors and steeple, with Carpenter Gothic decorations to enhance their church.

Ascension Anglican Church 1887

This Gothic Revival church in the village of Rushville has recently been preserved and restored to the useful purpose its beauty merits.

St. Peter's Church

This fine Gothic Revival church was built between 1875-1882 by the first German Lutheran congregation of Fairfield County, organized as early as 1805 by travelling missionaries from Pennsylvania. Services were held in German.
The church with its towering spire was reminiscent of German cathedrals and churches of the Gothic period. The beauty of the church is enhanced on the interior by the Chancel with its life size figures of Christ and the Apostles (close copies of those by Thorwaldsen in Copenhagen) and beautiful stained glass windows.

Gothic Revival chair found in one of Fairfield County's early homes.

St. Mary Church

Ten years in construction, 1854-1864, under the guidance of Father Lange, this fine structure of early Gothic style is the result of the genius, craftsmanship and perseverance of the local congregation. Guy and George Blair, well known stone masons, were in charge of construction and stone carving.
The beauty of the church is enhanced by very fine stained glass windows.

Detail of lancet window–carpenter Gothic gable trim.

With its steep gables in which are placed lancet windows of Gothic design, this small cottage achieves distinction. It is currently being restored.

Bonerigo – Shady 1863

Moore – Young – circa 1860

This century farm house combines a doorway of an earlier type with a Gothic gable and window.

Qualls – 1860

Charming cottage in Bremen combining some Greek revival and carpenter Gothic features.

Medill 1854

Wm. Medill, a native of the state of Delaware, came to Lancaster as a young lawyer in 1832. He soon embarked on a political career, first as the Fairfield County representative to the State Legislature, then to Congress for two terms, next as Ohio's first lieutenant governor of Ohio.

A bachelor, Mr. Medill build this small home in Lancaster while he was Governor, and whenever politics did not take him elsewhere, this was his home.

After being defeated for re – election in 1855, Medill was appointed Comptroller of the Treasury by President Buchanan. He had also previously served as Commissioner for Indian affairs.

This house is on the National Register.

Detail of a Gothic Revival window on a small cottage.

Carpenter Gothic trim often seen on small houses of the period.

Lehman
With its sharply pointed dormers and excellent scalloped bargeboard and decorations over the front door, this is a good example of a Carpenter Gothic cottage.

Vandervoort

Seltz–Dye

Two "German" type brick cottages.

Miller

Gothic door frame, door and mantel detail saved by a local preservationist when the old Latta house was torn down. It is his hope that some time a "Gothic" room can be reconstructed to exhibit this fine example of early Lancaster architecture. Lancet arches, quatrefoil design and crenelated moulding were all used.

A prize of coin silver, made from a Mexican silver dollar by a local silversmith, was awarded on Nov. 13, 1840 to Wm. Doty (who later became an artist and photographer) for superior conduct at the Lancaster Select English School.

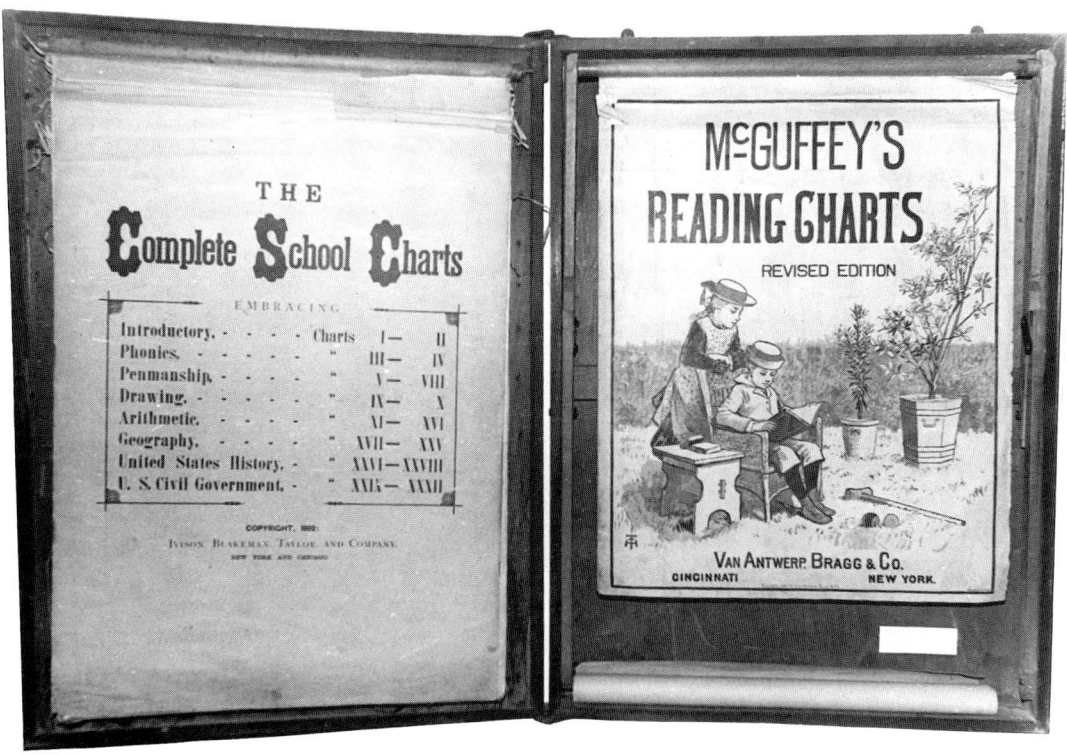

Large McGuffey charts were used to supplement the few books.

In an early one room country school house (now reconstructed on the fairgrounds) there were separate doors for boys and girls. Accommodating all grades, the children were kept warm with a huge pot-bellied stove.

Creed-Tallmadge-Nusser

This finest example of the Tuscan villa in Fairfield County was built in three stages. John M. Creed, a prominent Whig and ardent abolitionist built his home in the then newest, "Modern Italian Style" promoted in the East by architects of the time, but virtually unknown until the late 1830's in the Hocking Valley of Ohio. In addition, Mr. Creed had an office built just northeast of his home, in the even more ornate Gothic Revival style. He also had a large sandstone ice house, milk cellars, and huge basement for his barn built using dry masonry. It was complete with an underground tunnel from the barn to the basement of his home, which was used for hiding runaway slaves and helping them to get to the next stop on the underground railway at Rushville.

In 1847 John M. Creed died, at the age of thirty-eight, and soon after the house and farm was sold to Darius Tallmadge, who had recently purchased the Ohio Stage Coach Lines. He soon began enlarging the smaller Italianate style house into a full-scale Italian villa, copying designs by Richard Upjohn and Andrew Jackson Downing for the main entrance and square Tuscan tower to join the earlier house and office from where he directed the operations of the stage coach line.

Then he employed Russian and German gardeners and had fifteen acres of beautifully landscaped lawns with exotic trees and shrubs, flower gardens, vines, statuary, two fountains – all surrounded by a high iron fence. Along the turnpike was a pond containing several swans and in the center of the pond was a small island containing a rustic summer house.

To accommodate the throngs of Fairfield Countians who enjoyed strolling through his gardens on Sundays, Tallmadge constructed a willow-lined board-walk from the crossing of the canal to his garden gate. On the banks along this walk were planted vines of ever blooming roses and soon the area became known as Rosebank. Ever the businessman, Mr. Tallmadge charged a small fee for strolling across the board-walk to visit his magnificent gardens. Today's owners are occasionally surprised by the emergence of some long dormant exotic plant, a reminder of Tallmadge's landscape triumphs.

One of a pair of iron lions flanking the front entrance of the Tallmadge home.

Portrait of Mrs. Darius Tallmadge (Elizabeth Creed) in her wedding gown. Artist unknown.

Parlor of the Tallmadge-Nusser home with a pair of matching love seats original to the home.

Fine Victorian bed with heavy wooden canopy, original to the house.

Smith–Van Gundy

Built originally as a small Tuscan villa with the curved stone window hoods and square tower, it had a Victorian porch added. Somewhat later the house was covered with stucco.

Henry – 1865

Near Lancaster this farm house was built by the Henry family in the Tuscan villa style. With its four story square tower, curved stone and brick window hoods, several protruding bays, and bracketed cornices, it presents a very handsome appearance.

Weaving

There were a number of coverlet weavers in this part of Ohio, but the Heilbronns, father and son, were the most prolific here, advertising that they had the latest designs.

A beautiful coverlet by A. Allen has a most intricate and interesting design.

The hand woven carpeting in soft shades of red, green and beige, done on a jacquard loom, is quite lovely and rare.

Brock – Utley

This fine Italianate town house was built about 1860 by Daniel Sifford for his daughter. Originally it had a round tower with a metal spread eagle on top, which housed the "modern water system". The handsome marble mantels, chestnut woodwork with black walnut trim, spacious rooms, "in and out" windows from the drawing rooms to a triangular shaped veranda, mark it as a home for gracious living and entertaining.

A very handsome gilt pier mirror between windows in the drawing room reflects the fine chandeliers.

There are white marble mantels in the double drawing rooms. Here the very high ceiling can be noted.

McNeil–Peters–Reynolds 1860

In 1860, John D. Martin, who resided at that time in the Georgian, had this handsome Italianate type house built as a wedding present for his daughter, who married Dr. Robert McNeil, a prominent doctor. The bracketed cornice, the bay windows, the curved windows, the handsome drawing room with its unusual moulding are all typical of this period.

Detail of the fine stone window hoods of the McNeil–Peters–Reynolds home.

The flat roof with ornamental cornice supported by many brackets, the shaped window and door frames, the large rooms mark this house as one of the good Italianate houses in the Square Thirteen Historic Area.

Wetzler-Hurley 1870

Cox–Herrold 1850

This fine brick residence was built by Thomas Cox about 1850 at the corner of his large land holding. It is distinguished by its interesting wide bracketed cornice, stone window hoods and protruding bays. Thomas Cox was an ardent Democrat and copperhead. Clement Vallindingham, a leader of Ohio's copperheads, made this his headquarters when coming to Lancaster. The house was restored by Mr. and Mrs. Gordon Herrold.

The large ornate gilt mirrors over the two fireplaces were purchased in England for this house at the time it was built.

The curved stairway has an unusually fine carved newel post and spindles of black walnut and chestnut.

Orman-Weirich-Slater
Built by Henry Orman as a home for himself, the excellent wide cornice on this home gives it great distinction.

Green-Lollis-Bradford
The cornice of this brick home is distinguished by its bulls-eye ornamentation. The brackets and shaped window hoods are typical of the Italianate style, while the Ionic columns of the portico and porch hark back to the classic era.

Built for Charles Martin, one of Lancaster's most distinguished lawyers, who served two terms in Congress beginning in 1858, then returned to Lancaster to ably continue the practice of his profession in the local, state, and federal courts, this large house, with its original porches, bay stone lintels and bracketed cornice has been changed little in its restoration.

Martin-Deeds-Berens

This attractive brick town house, with its protruding bays, has a decorative overhanging protuberance which, with the portico, suggest the then popular stick style.

Rowlee–Householder

A transitional home of about 1860

Risch

143

Fairfield County Courthouse

The sandstone courthouse was built in 1871, designed in the Renaissance–Romanesque style with comparatively flat roof, a wide bracketed cornice, curved windows with ornamental window hoods. The sandstone was quarried locally, with George Blair and brothers being the stone masons. The fine iron fence was made by the Eagle Machine Co. – successors to the DeVol Foundry.

One of a series of eight murals of Fairfield County scenes painted in the "new" courthouse in 1871. Artist unknown.

On the keystone over the entrance to the 1870 courthouse is carved this stone face – said to be Henry Ebner, the St. Louis Architect for the courthouse.

Ruffner – Rowles Farm

This fine Italianate style house was built around 1860. Its unusually ornate brackets, the protruding entrance bay and many other details mark it as the very fine country home of a family who have occupied this land since 1806.

About 1805, Emanuel Ruffner and family came to Ohio from Virginia. The trip was made in a conestoga wagon, which served as their home until a cabin could be built.

A jack, made from a hollowed log, was useful in raising the wagon to repair a wheel.

Emanuel's 17-year-old son, Henry, was helping his father erect the cabin 1806, when he was killed by a tree he was felling, a not uncommon accident. He was buried in a plot on the farm, which is still maintained as a family burial ground.

The conestoga wagon in which the family first came to Ohio is still in the barn. Emanuel and his sons drove this wagon back east many times, stopping for supplies at Baltimore, Md. and Philadelphia. In 1832 the wagon was used by his son, Joseph–of Rushville, Ohio–so painted on the back board.

A primitive hand-made tin candle sconce was used in the early Ruffner cabin.

This hand-made flag was sewn by an early member of Emanuel Ruffner's family–Fairfield County's "Betsy Ross"–circa 1812, since there are eighteen stars. (However, there are only twelve stripes–she had probably used all the available red material.)

A little later this cabin was built. There the family resided until the large brick house was completed. Nearby is a spring house, and a large bank barn.

Huber–Jarik–Tolbert

Another unusually fine farm house has an almost lace like cornice with very decorative brackets. The window and door hoods are most ornate. Its very solid, but unsymmetrical mass marks it as one of the best houses of the period.

Inside the house the woodwork is a combination of black walnut and chestnut with the doors trimmed with stylized incised flowers.

Detail of one of the window hoods, showing rosette and acanthus leaf carving.

Allen–McKay– Donovan/Gale 1850

This exceptionally fine Italianate country home was built about 1850 by Lyman Allen, one of the sons of Dr. Silas Allen (scion of a distinguished New England family, descendants of John and Priscilla Alden) who with a company of forty neighbors traveled West and founded the village of Royalton.

A spiral stairway to the observation room, spacious rooms and interesting connected outbuildings in the New England manner, and the off center front door differentiate this house from many. This house is on the National Register of Historic Places.

Here is a fine empire type table, with a mirror below the marble top to view one's "petticoats". Above the table hangs a handsome empire mirror in which is reflected the brass and crystal candelabra.

Now occupied by the 5th, 6th and 7th generations of descendents of the original family who settled here in 1816, and lived in a log cabin near the present brick house. The double front doors of this early farm house are typical of those found in many parts of "Dutch" settled country.

One door leads into either a sitting room or kitchen and was in constant use. The other leads into the parlor and this one was unlocked for weddings, funerals, and spring and fall house cleaning only, – or possibly on Sunday if company came. Otherwise the house is generally of Italianate style, with the porch embellished with the carpenter's jig saw artistry.

Detwiler

The Julian family were earliest residents of Madison Township, coming from Berks County, Pa. in 1804. On their large farm they eventually built this fine 5 bay brick Italianate type house. Here the bracketed cornice is broken with a large curve over the center bay. At some later time a large addition with a two story porch was added. The original farm is still owned and operated by descendents.

Shartle – Julian

This fine farmhouse is in the process of restoration. Built over the classical center hall plan with a winding stair, it has the bracketed cornice, curved windows and low roof pitch of the Italianate type.

The original slate roof design adds much to the over all decorative effect. The interior woodwork, the curved doorway with its ruby glass are like other houses built about the same time by Isaiah Vorys, Jr.

Bowers-Shannon

Country Homes in the Italianate Style

Peters – Rockwood

The square masses of the design as well as the pairs of ornate brackets show a typical Italianate farm house, still lived in by descendents of the builder, Zebulon Peters.

Artz–Hughes–Lorenzi

High on a hill in Berne Township, this Italianate farm house was built by John Artz during the Civil War. His father, Jacob Artz, came to this location from Virginia in 1818. His mother was a sister of Nancy Hanks, Abraham Lincoln's mother. This home has large rooms with woodwork of chestnut, cherry and walnut. An interesting feature is the large semi-circular back porch.

An Italianate farm house has a very wide cornice with brackets and raised brick window hoods, a fine stairway, spacious rooms and an excellent ceiling plaster decoration in the hall.

Kirn–Bickham–Watts

Sherman House 1811, 1816, 1870

Ohio's only memorial to the Shermans is the Sherman House in Lancaster, a Registered National Historic Landmark commemorating the two Sherman brothers, General William Tecumseh and Senator John, who were born and spent their childhoods here.

Owned and operated by The Fairfield Heritage Association, the original 1811 section contains the restored dining room, master bedroom and children's bedroom; the 1816 section contains Judge Charles Sherman's study and the Sherman family parlor. On the second floor is a re-creation of General Sherman's field tent, a Civil war museum, and Sherman family memorabilia. The front Victorian section, pictured in the photo, was not associated with the Sherman occupancy which ended in 1844; it is furnished as a Victorian reception room, with a living room suite from General Sherman's New York apartment of the 1880's. Sherman House is open on a regular basis April through December and by appointment at other times.

Musser–Leitnaker 1865

This very large Italianate farm house was built for Henry Musser by Isaiah Vorys, Jr. Descendants still occupy the house and farm the original sections of land. Each side of the main house has five bays, with the bracketed cornices intersected at the N.S. and E. compass points by a curved pediment. The curves of the windows are reflected in the iron balustrade flanking the front entrance. The curved front doorway is surrounded with ruby glass ... "The house, summerhouse, and milkhouse cost $21,000. Grandfather said he didn't want to know what the barns and other buildings cost, but said he knew that it was too much ..."

This interesting milk house to the rear of the large house has a cupola with a bell to summon the family to meals. The iron work beside was originally part of the cresting on top of the house.

Henry Musser soon had an addition constructed to the rear of the house. This addition was surrounded by a large porch supported by eleven pillars.

In the cabin where the Musser family lived before the large house was built this early Fairfield County cherry four poster bed was used. The posters have decorative carved acorn finials. The trunk probably came to the county with the settlers.

Of interest, also, is the unusual double wash stand, with marble top and splash board.

The ornate Victorian buffet and handsome walnut bed were purchased in Cincinnati when this house was built and brought by canal boat to a near-by location.

Ewing – Daugherty – Tooill 1860

This large country home has all the elements of the 2nd Empire style: namely, slightly concave mansard roof with dormer windows, second story windows with classical pediments and bays and porches with decorative trim. There is a beautiful spiral stairway to the third floor and interior woodwork alternates butternut and black walnut. Nearby are brick spring and milk houses.

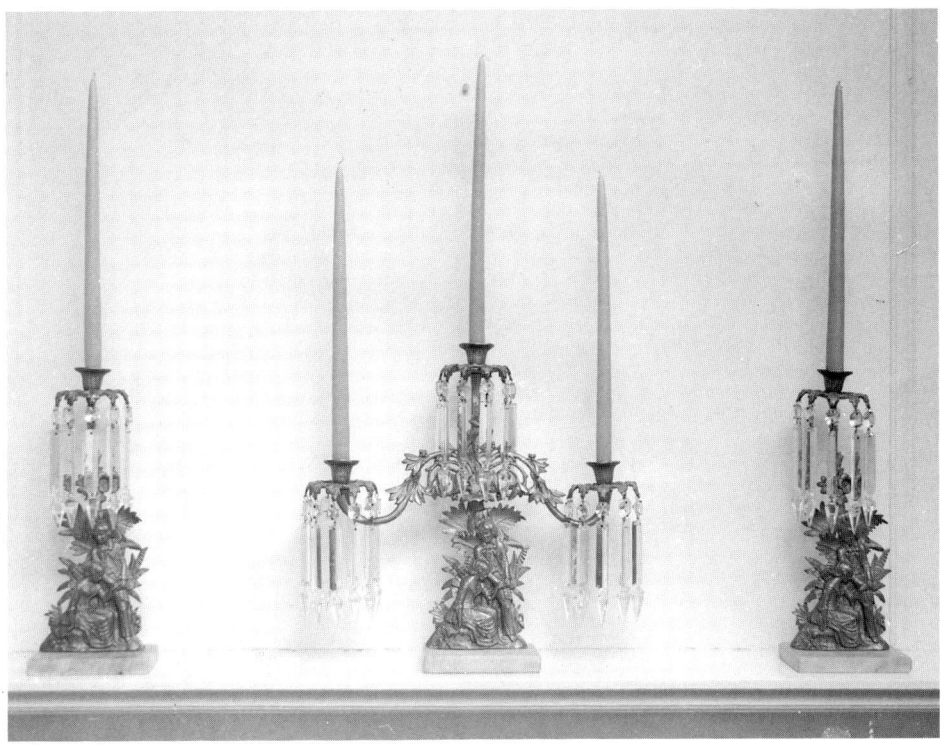

Handsome girandoles of brass, with crystal prisms to decorate a mantel, and light a room.

Rugh–Mast 1885

This excellent example of 2nd Empire style was constructed by a prosperous farmer. Adapted to a hillside location, it is notable for good proportion and slightly concave mansard roof crowned with delicate cresting. The lace-like cornice and cresting on the several porches as well as the curved stone window hoods and handsome two story bays, add to the elegant effect. This fine home merits restoration.

Sod cellar used by many farmers for storing vegetables in the winter. It always remains cool, but never freezes.

Maccracken–Coen–Ritchlin

First built by S. F. Maccracken as a Gothic Revival Cottage, this fine home was greatly enlarged by the addition of the third floor, with its stylish mansard roof, when purchased by Mr. Frederick C. Whiley for his family house. The square tower surmounted by decorative iron work was added to provide a water works system.

Brasee–Patterson–Dickinson 1865

The concave mansard roof with dormers, the protruding bays, a classical pediment crowning the window over the front doorway, the decorative detail of the porches mark this as a very elegant home of its period.

Hand carved walnut bellows.

Vorys–Walters–McCormick

This small brick home, complete with a square crested tower and slightly curvilinear roof, with rounded dormers to match those of the 2nd story, is a good example of the 2nd Empire style as locally construed.

Black–Probasco-Foura

A small country home exhibits three dormers on its mansard roof, and the lace-like trim on its roof and porch add greatly to its charm.

Younghaus–Champ–Tigner
1857

Pictured is the interesting mansard roof house built just prior to the Civil War by Justus Younghaus, who had a brewery on the Canal. It is thought he had a small wine cellar beneath the house. In 1871, John Snider, who had a large vineyard in the Kettle Hills area south of Lancaster, purchased the house and built a large wine cellar beneath. This sub-cellar is twenty five feet below the ground and maintains a temperature of 50° the year around. Snider leased his cellar which paralled High St. to the Hock-Hocking Wine Co., in 1872. In January of 1878, the American Wine Growers Association awarded a silver medal to the Hock-Hocking Cellars for the best American native wine.

The house with its large 15-feet-high rooms, graceful spiral stairway and walnut and chestnut woodwork, has undergone many changes over the years.

Original building

1994

Late Victorian
1870-1900

In the late decades of the 19th century, the styles of building became increasingly more involved and complicated, as the builders borrowed motifs from many types and combined them without restriction. They often devised original forms as seemed appropriate, with visual effect the desired end.

Picturesque Eclecticism was promoted by Charles Eastlake, an Englishman, who published seven editions of his handbook in this country. These featured flat, linear floral designs like jigsaw work in wood decorations and shallow incised patterns in stone. Eastlake's designs had a great influence on local craftsmen.

The other popular type of home design was known as the "Queen Anne", featuring protruding bay windows, tall and multiple shafted and decorated chimneys, assorted gables and rounded towers, projecting and receding porches, with a lavish mixture of materials and details. Umbricated shingles were commonly used in varying patterns to lend intricate, but subtle variations to the surface of the structure. Studied informality was characteristic of the period.

Toward the end of the century, the influence of Henry Hobson Richardson, recognized nationally as one of the great American architects, was felt here, particularly in large public buildings. These buildings of the *Richardson Romansque* era are easily distinguished by being built of rock-faced masonry, while arches and other structural features are emphasized by being smooth faced or of a different kind of stone. The effect of the large square towers with pyramidal roofs added to the general feeling of solidarity.

The ornate bronze fountain, a replica of one in Nantes, France, was made for and placed in the southwest section of Zane Square in 1890, to enhance the beauty of Lancaster's downtown.

Gill-Wright-Evans 1868

Following the Civil War, John Gill, a prosperous farmer and fine stock breeder, built this large home embodying all the latest style elements. He furnished it lavishly, for money spent on one's home, at that time, was not subject to capital tax. It is currently, and continuously, being restored by John, Marcia and Thane Evans who purchased the home from John Gill's descendants in 1988.

Still on the floor, in beautiful condition and color, is this original Wilton carpet.

The ornate chandelier featuring four coal oil lamps hung from an ornate plaster ceiling piece.

The little gazebo with its scalloped edges was an interesting feature of the garden.

Pugh-Kittle

One of the three finest Victorian houses in Walnut Township, this house was built by John Pugh; it faced the Ohio Canal, just below the Deep Cut. Its observation tower, small square windows just below the bracketed cornice, double chimney, walnut woodwork throughout, and spacious rooms make it an outstanding home.

The house built by J. E. Purvis in Bremen is a fine example of late Victorian exuberance. The focal point of the house is the cylindrical tower which has a decorative design. A porte-cochere, a second story porch, and a large semi-circular porch, as well as decorative tall chimneys mark this as the fine, substantial house of a man who had recently discovered oil in his community.

Purvis-Moyer

Keller

Farm home probably built during the late decades of the 19th century. It displays tower, bays, and dormers to make an interesting plan.

Late Victorian house, in the Historic District, showing the influence of Eastlake.

Martin-Parker -Barrett 1880

Ornately carved stone lintels and blocks on a Rushville home.

Decorative brackets, spindles, and jigsaw decorations adorn many late Victorian houses.

"Queen Anne" type town house complete with semi-octagonal oriel tower, high decorated chimney, umbricated shingles and decorative colored glass in the windows.

Shortly after the Civil War, Isaiah Vorys, Jr., a prolific builder, built this home for his own family. A few years later he added a protruding square tower complete with umbricated shingles in the latest Victorian style. This home was occupied by his descendents for 125 years after it was built.

Vorys-Drinkle-Taylor 1868

Stoneware jar, made for Mr. Charles Hammack about 1890. Mr. Hammack operated the Natural Gas Co. in the 1880's, and this is a portrait of him working with his gas pipes.

Picturesque horse's head hitching post, one of many made in one of Lancaster's early foundries, and still to be seen in front of several local homes.

Local Victorian Arts & Crafts

Iron coach dog–made in the 1880's by the Alten's foundry.

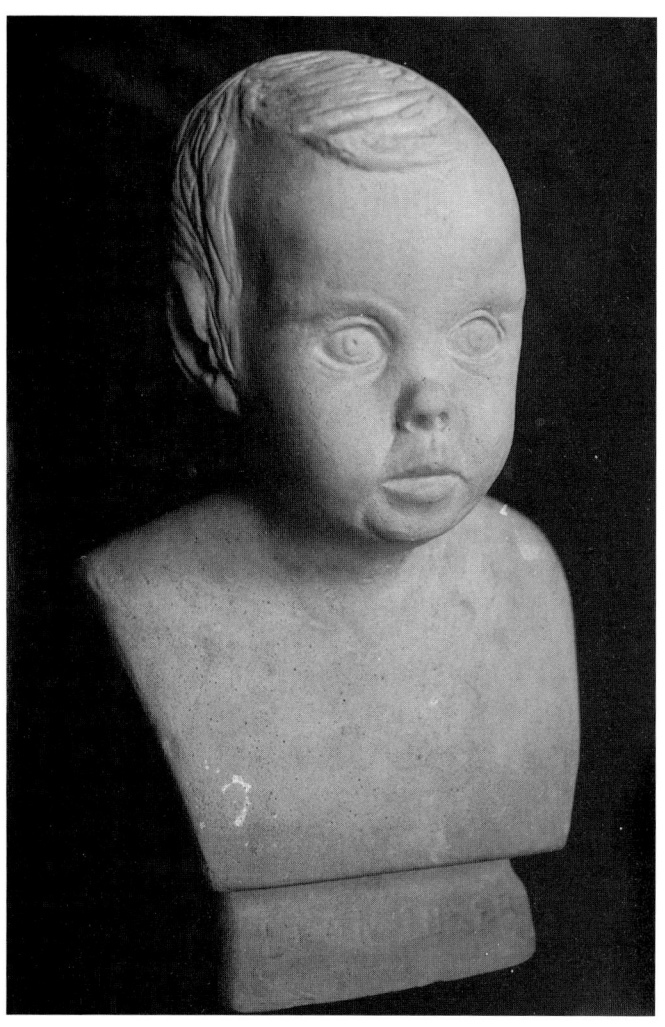

Dr. Gabriel Miesse, Jr., upon the untimely death of his only son, turned to the arts. He became known both as an accomplished pianist and prolific painter in the last decades of the 19th century. Several of his historical scenes were used to illustrate Hervey Scott's History of Fairfield County, published in 1876. He also painted many pastoral scenes and still life pictures.

In stone, Dr. Miesse sculpted this head of his young son, Leon Edgar. He was also a fine musician and composer, and his stirring march, "Mt. Pleasant Echoes" is still played occasionally by the United States Marine Band and others.

An 1870 Christmas card, which was done locally by E. S. Boem in calligraphy, (a much admired art form of penmanship) in the late Victorian era.

Turn of the Century Types

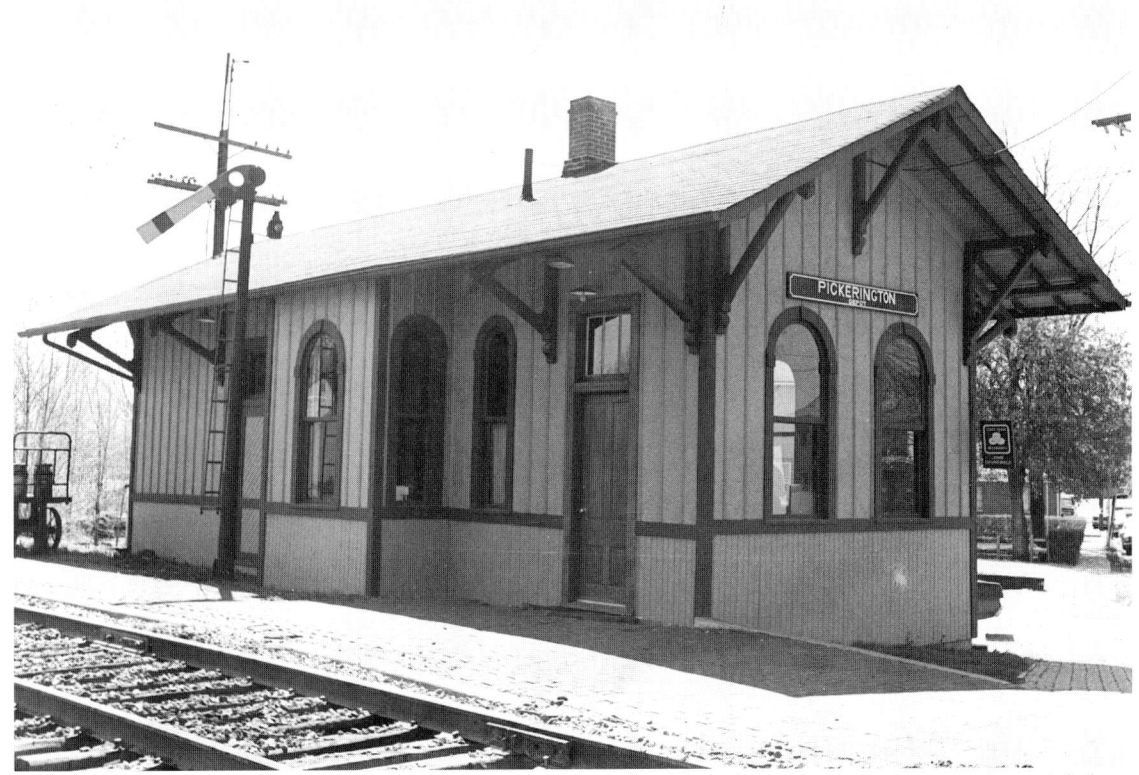

The interesting little railroad station in Pickerington is of board and batten construction with large overhanging eaves supported by stick style brackets.

In Bremen, Ohio, this United Methodist Church was built toward the end of the 19th century. With its steep hexagonal roof and gables, the square corner towers, curved stained glass windows, and umbricated shingles in a diamond design, it is an example of eclectic architecture.

The round cattle barn on the Fairfield County Fairgrounds built near the turn of the century is of unusual interest.

The curved construction of the wooden roof was a marvel in its day.

Just before the turn of the century, at what was then the Fairfield School for Boys, this large Neo-Classic Revival building was erected to house the Superintendent. Decorated elaborately for a 1960's Christmas display, this house is now used by the Ohio Department of Rehabilitation and Corrections as a training center for employees.

Neo-classic detail of this large home built about 1898.

Neeb-Heister-Oliver

At the Fairfield School for Boys, about 1895, this armory was built in the Richardson Romanesque style primarily. However, the two huge crenelated octagonal towers and pointed windows mark it as a late Gothic.

Downtown Business Buildings

Most of the commercial buildings on Lancaster's Main Street were built in the high Victorian period, and depict many styles.

This building with its exceptionally tall curved windows, its heavily bracketed cornice topped by an imposing broken arch is an example of Victorian eclecticism.

In this handsome building the stone quoins stress verticality. The stone window hoods and cornice are very decorative.

Mantel with sunburst design in one of Lancaster's earliest business buildings, built by John W. Giesy. While the first floor was used for business, the second and third floor housed The Golden Swan Tavern.

Although most of the downtown business buildings were built in the Victorian era, close observation shows the roof line and chimneys of an earlier classic period, in at least one building built by John W. Giesy. One can barely discern where a palladian window has been bricked in! The second and third floors exhibit fine craftsmanship in the stairs, dado, and mantels and merits restoration.

A fine Italianate five bay building, probably a single residence originally, but now in the commercial district.

In its perpendicular lines and ornamental brick work this building is Sullivanesque in feeling.

Detail of The Columbian building, once having a circular tower topped by a conical roof and decorated with a terra cotta frieze, can probably be best described as being basically Richardsonian Romanesque.

This cigar store Indian, hand carved from a single block of wood by Julius Melchers in the 1860's, is not a native of Fairfield County but now resides here. He is similar to several which stood on Main Street in the late Victorian era.

A stone building, with mansard roof, curved dormers and six very decorative curved windows on the second floor level is one of Lancaster's finest commercial buildings.

Rock Mill Covered Bridge is still in daily use. A short span, built in the 1880's over the gorge of the Hockhocking (Indian name for bottleneck), it is one of the most scenic. Rock Mill, for which it is named, was one of the earliest mills built in the county and operated by waterpower from the falls.

Looking across Zane Square, past the Civil War cannon which General Wm. T. Sherman gave to his home town, we see the "new" City Hall. It is built in the style so popular at the time for large public buildings – Richardsonian-Romanesque. Its rough faced locally quarried stone, curved arches and windows emphasized by smooth faced stone, tall square tower crowned with a steep pyramidal roof, prominent roof dormers are all characteristic of this style. (At last the citizens of Lancaster were to have the town clock which they so long ago had petitioned unsuccessfully to have put in the tower of the Presbyterian church.)

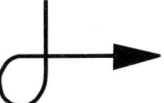

Bibliography

Benjamin, Asher. *The American Builder's Companion*, R. P. & C. Williams. 1827

Bolton, Ethel Stanwood. *Wax Portraits and Silhouettes.*

Coleman, Dorothy Ent. *Greek Revival Architecture of Lancaster, Ohio.*

Cook, Lewis. *Recollections of Fairfield County.*

Contosta, David. *19th Century Architecture of Lancaster, Ohio.*

Frary, I. T. *Early Houses of Ohio.*

Gowans, Alan. *Images of American Living.* Lippincott & Co. 1964

Hamlin, Talbot. *Greek Revival Architecture in America.* Dover Publications. 1944

Hutslar, Donald A. *Log Architecture of Ohio.*

Knittle, Rhea Mansfield. *Ohio Frontier Series* No. I. 1937

Knittle, Rhea Mansfield. *Early Ohio Taverns.* 1937

Knittle, Rhea Mansfield. *Early Ohio Silversmiths and Pewterers.*

Leitnaker, Musser. *Records of the Leitnaker Family.*

McKee, Harley J. *Introductions to Early Ohio Masonry.* National Trust for Historic Preservation and Columbia University. 1973

Miller, C. C. *History of Fairfield County*

Morison, Samuel Elliot. *History of the American People.* Oxford University Press. 1965

Richter, Conrad. *The Awakening Land.* Alfred A. Knopf. 1973

Ruffner, Doris Laver and Ruffner, Oliver Taylor. *Peter Ruffner and his Descendents.* 1966

Sanderson, George. *Early Settlement of Fairfield County.* Thomas Wetzler, Lancaster. 1851

Scott, Hervey. *History of Fairfield County.* Siebert and Lilley. 1877

Siebert, Wilbur Henry. *The Mysteries of Ohio's Underground Railroads.*

Swett, Chester, M. D. *Medicine in Fairfield County,* 1800-1850.

Turnbull, Donald C. *History of the First Presbyterian Church.*

Weiser, Fredricks and Howell B. Henvey. *Pennsylvania German Fractur of the Free Library of Philadelphia.*

Whiffen, Marcus. *American Architecture since 1780.* M.I.T. Press. 1969

Wiseman, C.M.L. *Centennial History of Lancaster, Ohio* F. J. Heer. 1898

Wiseman, C.M.L. *Pioneers of Fairfield County, Ohio* F. J. Heer. 1901

Wust, Klaus, *Virginia Fraktur.*

INDEX

Adams (house detail), 92
Allen, A., 134
Allen, Lyman, (house), 149
Allen, Dr. Silas, 149
Alten's foundry, 169
American Legion, 80-81, 91
Anchor Guest House, 74-76
Arnold, Daniel, 20; Elizabeth, 16;
   Frederick, 20; Henry, 20
Artz, Jacob, 151; John (house), 151
Ascension Anglican Church, 118

Baker, Daniel, 35, 105, 112
Baldwin, John, 68
Barr (house), 107
Barrett (house), 167
Beecher, Philemon, 19
Beery (house), 110
Benjamin, Asher, 35, 36, 56
   62, 81
Berens (house), 143
Betzer, Eliza, 133
Bickham, John (house), 151
Bilderback, Charles, 26
Black (house), 161
Blair, George, 94, 119, 144;
   Guy, 94, 119; Henry, 94
Boem, E. S., 170
Bonerigo (house), 120
Bope, Abraham (house detail), 108
Bope's Corner, 25, 70, 108
Bowers (house), 150
Boyd, 70
Bradford (house), 142
Brasee, Alice, 103; John T., 103
Brasee (house), 160
Bremen United Methodist Church, 171
Bright, Amos G., 33
Bright (house), 107
Brock (house), 136-137
Brown (house), 94
Brumfield (house), 95
Budden (house), 111
Burns (house), 78
Bush, Samuel, 20, 85
Bush (house), 85

Carpenter, (family), 31
Casper, 86
Cassell, Wm., 35, 50, 64
Champ (house), 162

Chestnut Ridge, 114-115
Church, Isaac, 35, 84
Clark (house), 82
Clark, Joshua, 35
Claspill, George, 76
Cluff (house), 44
Coates, Samuel, Jr., 6; Samuel, Sr., 6, 10, 98
Coen (house), 159

Concord Hall, 92, 102-104
Cooper, Robert, 6
Courthouse, Fairfield County (first),
   17, 18; "new", 144
Cox, Thomas (house), 140-141
Cox, Tunis (house), 58
Creed (house), 62, 81, 128-131
Creed, John, 98, 128
Crites (house), 106
Crumley (Gramlich), Christian, 29;
   Conrad, 29
Culp (house), 111

Dallow, Joseph, Mrs., 75, 76
Dallow (house), 74-76
Daugherty, (house), 156-157
Davis (house), 107
Deeds (house), 143
Deppe, Julius (house), 77
Detweiler (house), 150
DeVol, Gilbert, 72, 74; Jonathan, 74
DeVol Foundry, 72, 144
DeVol (house), 74-76
Dickinson (house), 160
Dietrick, Jacob D., 28
Donovan/Gale (house), 149
Doty, Wm., 125
Downing, Andrew J., 127
Drinkle (house), 168
Duffield, Wm., 35
Dumm (house), 83
Duncan, Mary, 58
Dye (house), 125

Eastlake, Charles, 163, 167
Eagle Machine Co., 144
Edstrom (house), 109

Effinger (house), 53-55, 68, 75, 76
Effinger, Edward, 54; Dr. Michael, 55; Samuel, 30, 53; Tella, 54
English Lutheran Church, 116
Evans (house), 164-165
Ewing-Daugherty-Tooill (house), 156-157
Ewing-Kirn-Ryckman (house), 46, 47
Ewing, Philomen, 60; Thomas, 19, 22, 46, 60, 99

Fairfield County Fairgrounds, 172
Fairfield Heritage Association, 64, 152
Fairfield School for Boys, 173, 174
Fenwick, Father, 19
Ferguson, Wm. F., 79
Ferguson (house), 79
Finley, James 17
Foura (house), 161
Fox (house), 102-104
Franklin (house), 108
Fromlet (family), 51
Furniss (house), 79

Gale (house), 149
Garaghty, Michael, 56
Garaghty-Mumaugh (house), 56-57
Gates, 86
George (house), 12
Georgian, The, 54, 63-70
Giani (house), 19
Giesy, John W., 176
Gill, John (house), 164-165
Graybill, Samuel, 33
Green (house), 142
Green, Allen, 6; John, 6, 26; Ruhama, 26
Grey, Nellie, 105
Grubb, Joseph, 74
Gurile/Schwartz (house), 85
Guthrie (house), 96

Hamlin, Talbot, 49
Hammack, Charles, 169
Hampson, James, 18, 35
Hanby, Benjamin, 105; Reverend, 105
Harmon, Frederick, 11, 12, 13
Harmon (house), 12
Heilbronn, George, 133, J. J., 134
Heisey (house), 77
Heister (house), 174
Henry (house), 132
Hermann, John, 28, 29, 30
Herrold, Gordon (house), 140-141
Holcombe, Burrowes, 99
Householder (house), 143
Hoyt, Mary, 22
Huber (house), 148
Huddle (house), 82
Hughes (house), 151

Hummel (house detail), 81
Hunnewill, 53
Hunter, Hocking, 6, 58, 79; John, 58; Captain Joseph, 6
Hunter (house), 58
Hurley (house), 139
Hyde, Dr. Simon, 25, 92, 105
Hyde (house details), 92, 105

Irvin, Judge Wm., 19

Jarik (house), 148
Jones, Inigo, 61
Julian (house), 150

Keller (house), 166
Kemmerer, Joseph, 30
Kindler, J., 41
Kirn (Ewing-Kirn-Ryckman house), 46, 47
Kirn-Bickham-Watts (house), 151
Kistler (house), 107
Kittle (house), 166
Kocher (house), 83
Kraner (house), 111
Krebs, F., 29
Kutz, David and Rebecca, 51

Lancaster City Hall, 178-179
Lange, Father, 119
Lanning (house), 95
Latta (house details), 125
Lehman (house), 124
Leist, John, 35-44
Leist-Cluff-Weinberg (house), 44-45
Leist-Mathias-Strausbaugh (house), 43
Leist-Smith (house), 40-42
Leist-Veffer (house), 37-39
Leitnaker (house), 153-155
Lollis (house), 142
Lorenzi (house), 151
Love (house), 105

Maccracken-Coen-Ritchlin (house), 159
Maccracken, Samuel F., 63, 64, 67, 68, 70; Sarah, 67, 68
Market House, 21
Marquette (house), 32
Martin, Charles, 143; John D., 65, 138; Mary Jane, 58
Martin-Deeds-Berens (house), 143
Martin-Parker-Barrett (house), 167
Masonic Temple, 21, 84
Mast (house), 158
Mathias (house), 43

Matlack (house), 19
Matlack (family), 97
Matlack-Burns-Roche (house), 78
Mattox (house), 71-72
Mayer, David (house and barn), 32
McCabe, Sothenes, 18
McCandlish, Agnes, 16
McCormick (house), 161
McDonald (house), 106

McKay (house), 149
McMullen, Joseph, 6
McNeil, Robert, 16; (house), 138-139
Medill (house), 122; Gov. Wm., 122
Melchers, Julius, 177
Methodist Church, First, 60; 84
Metzger (house), 106
Meyer (house), 110
Miers, Henry, 35
Miesse, Dr. Gabriel, Jr., 170; Leon Edgar, 170
Miller-Beery (house), 110
Miller, W. C. (house), 125
Mithoff, Augustus, 104
Monger (house), 87-88
Moore (house), 121
Morgan (house), 111
Morrow (house), 32
Mt. Tabor Church, 17
Mt. Zion Methodist Church, 117
Moyer (house), 166
Mumaugh (house), 19, 52, 56-57
Mumaugh, Fannie, 56
Musser (house), 153-155
Musser, Henry, 153, 154

Neeb (house), 174
Noble, John, 34; Mary, 17
Nolan (house), 79
Nusser (house), 128-131

Ogilvie (house), 83
Oliver (house), 174
Orman, Henry, 35
Orman (house), 142
Osterhage (house), 83
Outcault, Richard, 58, 59

Parker (house), 167
Patterson (house), 160
Perkins (house) 106
Peters (Reese-Peters house), 46-52;
   (McNeil-Peters-Reynolds house), 138-139
   Peters-Rockwood (house), 151
   Zebulon, 151
Pleasant Hill Church, 12
Presbyterian Church, Second, 84

Probasco (house), 161
Pugh, John (house), 166
Purvis, J. E. (house), 166
Putnam, Rufus, 33

Quinn, Rev. James, 17
Qualls (house), 121

Reber, Valentine, 40, 41
Reed, John B., 51, 77
Reese-Peters (house), 46-52
Reese, Henry, 71; William, 19, 46, 71
Reynolds (house), 138-139
Richardson, Henry, 163
Ridley (house), 82
Risch (house), 143
Rising, Russell (house), 60-62
Ritchlin (house), 159
Roche (house), 78
Rock Mill, 178
Rockwood (Reese-Mattox-Rockwood
   house), 71; Peters-Rockwood (house), 151
Romano (house), 82
Rowlee (house), 143
Rowles (house), 145-147
Ruffner (house), 145-147
Ruffner, Emanuel, 145, 146, 147;
   Henry, 146; Joseph, 146
Rugh (house), 158
Rushville United Methodist Church, 112
Ryckman (house), 46-47

St. John's Episcopal Church, 114, 116
St. Mary Catholic Church, 119
St. Paul's Lutheran Church, 112
St. Peter's Lutheran Church, 118
Sanderson, George, 10, 28, 35
Savery, William, 48
Scholl (house), 111
Schultz (house), 83
Schwartz (house), 85
Scott, Hervey, 170
Selby, Joe, 105
Seltz (house), 125
Shady (house), 120
Shaeffer (house), 114-115
Shaeffer, Edward, 28; Frederick, 114; Isaac, 6
Shannon (house), 150
Shartle (house), 150
Shaw's Inn, 30, 53
Sherman House Museum, 22-23, 152
Sherman, Charles, 22, 23, 46, 152;
   Ellen Ewing, 78; John, 23, 152;
   Mary, 22, 46; Mary Elizabeth, 46, 71;
   Gen. William Tecumseh, 23, 78, 152, 178
Sifford-American Legion (house), 80-81, 91

185

Sifford-Osterhage-Ogilvie (house), 83
Sifford, Daniel, 64, 74, 80, 81, 83, 116, 135
Slater (house), 142
Smith (Leist-Smith house), 40-42
Smith (Blair-Brown-Smith house), 94
Smith (Baker-Love-Smith house), 105
Smith-Van Gundy (house), 132
Snider, John, 162
Spires (house), 82
Spook Hollow, 85
Stanbery-Rising (house), 60-62, 103
Stanbery, Henry, 19, 60
Standing Stone (Mt. Pleasant), 13
Stenson (house), 106
Stebelton, Max, 7, 8
Stepilton, Joseph, 101
Stonewall Cemetery, 89
Stout-Adams (house detail), 92
Stout-Metzger-Perkins (house), 106
Strausbaugh (house), 43
Strentz, Wendell, 90
Strickler, John, 90, 93
Stuckey (house), 96
Sturgeon, Thomas, 26, 27, 86; Timothy, 26, 27
Stutzman (house), 111

Tallmadge (house), 128-131
Tallmadge, Darius, 128, 129, 130; Elizabeth Creed, 130
Taylor (house), 168
Teal, Patience, 17
Tecumseh, 22
Terry, Eli, 101
Thomas (house), 109
Thurston Baptist Church, 112
Tigner (house), 162
Toellerin, Magdalena, 29
Tolbert (house), 148
Tooill (house), 156-157
Triance (house), 96
Tucker, Elisha, 54, 70
Turner, Herbert (house), 85

Upjohn, Richard, 127
Utley (house), 136-137

Vandervoort (house), 124
Van Gundy (house), 132
Van Pearse (house), 96
Van Roden, Magdalena, 40
Van Trump, Philadelphus, 19
Veffer (house), 37
VonRoden, Agatha, 103, 104
Vorys-Drinkle-Taylor (house), 168
Vorys-Walters-McCormick (house), 161
Vorys (Sifford-Vorys-Wiseman-American Legion house), 80-81, 91
Vorys, A. I., 80; Isaiah, Jr., 150, 153, 168, Isaiah, Sr., 28, 35, 56, 73

Voss (house), 114-115
Walters (house), 161
Waterloo Tavern, 110
Watts (house), 151
Weakley, J. A., 35, 84
Weaver, Christopher, 35
Weinberg (house), 44-45
Weirich (house), 142
Welsh (house), 58
Wetzler (house), 139
Whiley, Frederick C., 159
Whitman (house), 96
Will, John, 95
Williamson, John, 18, 35, 56
Wilson (house), 87-88
Wilson, Gustin, 89; Nathaniel, 6, 87, 88, 89
Wiseman, C. M. L., 80, 116
Witte (house), 102-104
Witte Augustus, 102, 103, Agatha Von Roden, 104 Cecilia, 104, George, 103
Woltz, Jesse, 64, 86
Work, Edgar, 27; John, 27
Wright, Rev. John, 17, 19
Wright (house), 164
Wyandot Indians, 112

1. COURT HOUSE.
2. CITY HALL & P.O.
3. HOTEL MARTIN.
4. TEMPLE of FASHION & BEE HIVE BLOCK.
5. OPERA HOUSE
6. MITHOFF HOUSE
7. GERMAN LUTHERAN CHURCH
8. PRESBYTERIAN "
9. EPISCOPAL CHURCH.
10. IMMANUELS LUTHERAN CHURCH.
11. CATHOLIC "
12. METHODIST "
13. COLORED M.E. "
14. ENGLISH LUTHERAN "
15. OLD GERMAN "
16. EVANGELICAL "

LANC

Q. H. BAILEY & CO.